LIBERATING
PLANET EARTH

Other books by Gary North

Marx's Religion of Revolution, 1968
An Introduction to Christian Economics, 1973
Unconditional Surrender, 1981
Successful Investing in an Age of Envy, 1981
The Dominion Covenant: Genesis, 1982
Government by Emergency, 1983
The Last Train Out, 1983
Backward, Christian Soldiers?, 1984
75 Bible Questions Your Instructors
    Pray You Won't Ask, 1984
Coined Freedom: Gold in the Age of
    the Bureaucrats, 1984
Moses and Pharaoh, 1985
Negatrends, 1985
The Sinai Strategy, 1986
Unholy Spirits: Occultism and
    New Age Humanism, 1986
Conspiracy: A Biblical View, 1986
Honest Money, 1986
Fighting Chance, 1986 [with Arthur Robinson]
Dominion and Common Grace, 1987
Inherit the Earth, 1987
Is the World Running Down?, 1987
The Pirate Economy, 1987
Liberating Planet Earth, 1987
    (Spanish) *Teología de Liberación*, 1987
Healer of the Nations, 1987

Books edited by Gary North

Foundations of Christian Scholarship, 1976
Tactics of Christian Resistance, 1983
The Theology of Christian Resistance, 1983
Editor, *Journal of Christian Reconstruction* (1974-1981)

LIBERATING PLANET EARTH

An Introduction to
Biblical Blueprints

Gary North

Dominion Press
Ft. Worth, Texas

Published by Dominion Press
7112 Burns Street, Ft. Worth, Texas 76118

Typesetting by Thoburn Press, Tyler, Texas

Printed in the United States of America

Unless otherwise noted, all Scripture quotations are from the New King James Version of the Bible, copyrighted 1984 by Thomas Nelson, Inc., Nashville, Tennessee.

Library of Congress Catalog Card Number 87-071021

ISBN 0-930462-51-3

This book is dedicated to
Loren Cunningham
whose Youth With A Mission
is doing so much to liberate
people from the bondage of sin.

TABLE OF CONTENTS

For political religions, for humanism, evil is in the environment, and the state's power to change that environment is its saving grace. The state must remake man's physical and spiritual environment in order to change and save man. Social change in terms of the state's plan is statist grace in operation. The bad environment must be destroyed in order to free man. This evil environment sometimes involves persons and institutions, such as the bourgeousie, capitalists, the clergy, Christians, churches, private organizations, private enterprise, and so on. All these may have to be, and frequently are, "liquidated" or destroyed as part of the process of salvation. Those persons remaining must be "re-educated" in terms of the new creed and out of Christianity.

For Biblical Christianity, the answer to the problem of evil is God's grace, the grace of God through Jesus Christ and the restitution of all things. Man's problem is not his environment but *sin*, man's desire to be his own god, his own law and principle of ultimacy. Man cannot save himself, either by politics, works of law or morality, or by any other means. Jesus Christ is man's only savior. Man must live under God's law order in order to live freely and happily, but the law order cannot save man, nor will that law order long survive, if there be not a sizable body of believers whose life is the law of God. Basic to true order therefore is grace. Without grace, man lacks the character to develop his potentialities, capitalize his activities, and order his life.

R. J. Rushdoony*

*Rushdoony, *The Foundations of Social Order* (Fairfax, VA: Thoburn Press [1968] 1978), pp. 222-23.

INTRODUCTION

Then Jesus said to those Jews who believed on Him, "If you abide in My word, you are My disciples indeed. And you shall know the truth, and the truth shall make you free" (John 8:31-32).

I originally wrote this book as an evangelical tool to be used primarily by Spanish-speaking Christians in their struggles against atheism, Communism, and the popular socialist religion known as liberation theology. Nevertheless, this book is more than an anti-Communist tract. We must be more than anti-Communists. We must be able to offer a comprehensive, workable alternative to Communism. Nothing less than this will be successful. Marxism is the most consistent and powerful secular religion of all time; it can only be successfully challenged by an even more consistent and more powerful Biblical religion.

I realized that the book could also serve English-speaking people as an introduction to Christianity—not the traditional "one hour and three prayers per week" sort of Christianity, but the Christianity of the Bible. This Christianity presents a *comprehensive challenge* to the modern world, and it also offers *comprehensive solutions* to the complex problems of our day.

Christianity has not survived for almost two thousand years because it is culturally irrelevant. It captured and then transformed the dying Roman Empire in the fourth century. It laid the foundations of modern science during the late medieval period (1000-1500), and developed it in the early modern period (1500-1700). Kings governed in the name of Christianity, and others were overthrown in the name of Christianity. It is proper to speak of Christian civilization, but for well over a century, such language has seemed

1

out of date. And so it is, for our civilization today is humanistic, not Christian. This is the heart of mankind's problems.

The Road to Serfdom

In 1944, an Austrian economist living and teaching in Great Britain published a remarkable book, *The Road to Serfdom*. His name is F. A. Hayek. As I write these words, he is still alive and vigorous at age 88, working to complete his three-volume study of modern socialism, *The Fatal Conceit*.

The book received little attention in Great Britain, but in that same year, the *Reader's Digest* published a condensation of it. He sailed to the U.S. as an obscure economist; he arrived as a celebrity. It was *The Road to Serfdom*, more than any other single publication, that launched the revival of free market economics in the English-speaking world.

The book's thesis was simple: it is impossible to preserve freedom under an economy that is run by the State. If the State can take your money, or the fruits of your labor, then it can leave you without the means of pursuing your own personal earthly goals. Democratic socialism is still socialism, he concluded, and voting rights alone will not preserve freedom if men are not allowed to keep most of the fruits of their labor, including intellectual labor.

This argument created outrage among democratic socialists all over the world. But decade by decade, Hayek's warning has begun to be taken seriously by a growing minority of scholars. His predictions about the failure of government economic planning have steadily come true. By 1980, six years after he had won the Nobel Prize in economics, he could no longer keep up with the books, essays, and other publications written about his ideas. At an age when most men have been retired for a quarter century, Hayek is still going strong.

Is the West still walking the wrong way down the road to serfdom? Yes. Even the various national conservative and "libertarian" revivals have not reversed the overall trend, nor can they. The reason is simple: *only through faith in Jesus Christ can any society discover, develop, and maintain the legal institutions that make freedom possible.*

This is a strong statement, but it is one of the key doctrines of the Bible. Can people who are slaves of sin escape other forms of slavery? The Bible's answer is clear: *no*. Eventually bondage to sin produces earthly forms of bondage. This was the lesson of the Book of Judges, as well as First and Second Kings. To escape bondage, people must first escape bondage to sin, the original bondage.

What we need is to turn around and go back the other way. *The road to serfdom is a two-way street*. In the Bible, the word "repent" means "turn around." Through the grace of God, people are able to repent:

> For by grace have you been saved through faith, and that not of yourselves; it is the gift of God, not of works, lest anyone should boast (Ephesians 2:8-9).

People can be transformed morally, and this alone enables them to overcome this world. By coming under the covenant that God makes with His people, Christians can play a role in overcoming the many evils of this world.

Regeneration by grace through faith in Jesus Christ is the first step on the road *from* serfdom. It is the first step in liberation.

Liberation Theology

This is a book about liberation theology. In fact, it's a book about two radically different types of theology, each of which claims to be preaching liberation. One of these systems is Marxist, and the other is Christian. One is based on the teachings of a man who claimed that religion is the opium (drug) of the people, while the other is based on the teachings of a perfect man who was also the incarnation of God Himself.

We must be clear about this from the beginning. Karl Marx, the founder of the political movement known as Communism, was an atheist. He had been a liberal Christian as a youth, as we can see in his schoolboy essay, "On the Union of the Faithful with Christ according to John XV, 1-14."[1] But by age 20, he had aban-

---

1. Reprinted in Robert Payne (ed.), *The Unknown Karl Marx* (New York: New York University Press, 1971), pp. 39-43.

doned his belief in God. In an essay he wrote in 1843, at age 25, Marx said: "Religion is the sigh of the oppressed creature, the sentiment of a heartless world, and the soul of soulless conditions. It is the *opium* of the people."[2] In that same essay, he argued for humanism, the idea that mankind is the highest form of being—in other words, that man is god. "The criticism of religion ends with the doctrine that *man is the supreme being for man*."[3] Again, "The emancipation of Germany is only possible *in practice* if one adopts the point of view of that theory according to which man is the highest being for man."[4] (The emphases were his; I have added nothing.)

We now know what Marx was: an atheistic humanist. What about Jesus? What did Jesus say about Himself? At His trial before the Jewish leaders, the high priest asked Him: "Are you the Christ, the Son of the Blessed?" The Jews did not mention the name of God; they used such words as "Blessed" as substitutes. Jesus knew what He was being asked: "Are you the Son of God?" He replied:

"I am. And you will see the Son of Man sitting at the right hand of Power, and coming with the clouds of heaven." Then the high priest tore his clothes and said, "What further need do we have of witnesses? You have heard the blasphemy! What do you think?" And they all condemned Him to be worthy of death (Mark 14:61-64).

Jesus' words *were* blasphemy, *unless* He really was the Son of God. By Hebrew law, He *was* worthy of death (Leviticus 24:16), *unless* He really was the Son of God. By His resurrection from the dead (Matthew 28) and His ascension to heaven (Acts 1:9-11) to stand at the right hand of God (Acts 7:56), He proved that He was what He said He was. He was God walking on earth. He said plainly, "I and My Father are one" (John 10:30).

---

2. Karl Marx, "Contribution to the Critique of Hegel's Philosophy of Right," in T. B. Bottomore (ed.), *Karl Marx: Early Writings* (New York: McGraw-Hill, 1964), pp. 43-44.
3. *Ibid.*, p. 52.
4. *Ibid.*, p. 59.

Jesus said that belief in Him as the Son of God is a life-and-death issue. It is an *eternal* life-and-death issue.

> The Father loves the Son, and has given all things into His hand. He who believes in the Son has everlasting life; and he who does not believe the Son shall not see life, but the wrath of God abides on him (John 3:35-36).

There can be no compromise here. It is either faith in God or faith in man. It is either Christianity or Marxism. There is no honest and accurate way to put Marxism together with Christianity. These two deeply religious systems are at war with each other. Marx understood this completely. This war will not end until either Christianity perishes—and it will never perish—or Marxism perishes. Anyone who attempts to put these two systems together into one system is either self-deceived or else a conscious agent of the Communists, who is seeking to deceive others. He is either ignorant or evil.

Religion as a Tool of Communism

The popular religious system known today as liberation theology is an attempt to combine the revolutionary Communism of Karl Marx and the language of certain passages in the Bible that make it sound as if the Bible preaches Communism's bloody revolution and socialism. This humanistic version of the Bible's message of liberation never mentions either the divinity of Christ or the perfect humanity of Jesus Christ (which is different from His divinity), or salvation by faith in Christ alone, or the requirement of Christians to obey lawful authorities, or the transforming power of the gospel, or the transforming power of God's Holy Spirit, or the continuing requirements of God's law, or God's covenants with mankind, or the eighth commandment ("You shall not steal"), or the tenth commandment ("You shall not covet"), or dozens of other basic themes in the Bible. The Marxists do not believe in a God who created this world and will bring it to final judgment. They believe only in man.

Why, then, have they adopted liberation theology? Three

reasons suffice: (1) the normal Communist practice of deception; (2) the need to infuse stagnating Marxist thought with a new religious impulse; (3) the realization that it is a high-risk strategy to impose atheism on a religious society prematurely. Let's look at each of these.

1. Deception

It is easier to enlist the support of the average citizen if you disguise your intention to destroy everything he holds dear. The Communists are out to destroy Western Civilization. Marx said so from the beginning. Western Civilization is middle class—"bourgeois"—and the Communists hate it even as they imitate it and buy Western goods.

Satan is a deceiver. He prefers to use deception. He deceived Eve. He deceived the nations. He used Biblical citations in his major temptations (Genesis 3:1; Matthew 4:6).

2. A Dying Faith

In Communist nations, Marxism is a dead religion. It is a joke. The idea that Marxism-Leninism is taken seriously in the Soviet Union or Communist China is a myth indulged in only by a shrinking number of Western intellectuals.

What Communism has produced is an endless series of crop failures. In Communist China, it took only two years of partial free market agriculture to make that nation an exporter of food, 1983-85, after four decades of starvation. Communism is also the most efficient producer of bureaucratic inefficiency in history. It produces bumper crops of cynicism and corruption. Communist nations systematically and deliberately corrupt their populations. Guilt-ridden, corrupt populations are easier to control.

The Communists know they can compete with the West only in terms of sheer military and terrorist power. Those are their specialty exports in the world economy.

When a religion begins to lose its followers, it must reform itself or else resort to power and fear to remain dominant. The final stages of a religion are seen when its followers no longer believe its creeds, but instead seek to escape from it: by drunkenness, escape, or corruption.

At this stage in Marxism's history, the Communists must find new sources of ethical motivation and vision. The Bible gives them the rhetoric of moral vision that they need.

3. Quest for New Allies

In 1965, there was a revolt by Communist forces in Indonesia against the tottering socialist government of President Sukarno. This revolt failed. In the wave of Muslim wrath that followed, at least 200,000 Communists and their suspected supporters were slaughtered. It may have been as many as a million.

The Communists learned an important lesson: it is risky to try to impose an alien atheist religion on deeply religious people. They adopted a new strategy: a far more open, less clandestine cooperation between Communism and religion. From 1965 on, the Communists began to promote a "Marxist-Christian dialogue." These were one-sided affairs; the Communists conceded nothing, and the people who dealt with them—humanists who called themselves Christians—conceded everything. The most widely known Communist in this dialogue was French scholar Roger Garaudy. When he opposed publicly the Soviet invasion of Czechoslovakia in 1968, he was expelled from the French Communist Party. So much for "dialogue" and "the mutual sharing of views."

Conservative Christian journalist and historian Otto Scott has commented on the importance of the Indonesian slaughter for international Communist strategy:

> Turning toward Central and South America, they realized that a revolution could not achieve success in those regions unless it included religious elements. Consequently, their Hispanic campaign moved beyond the intellectuals (a corrupt element available to any purchaser at any time) and into traditional Roman Catholic circles. Liberation theology was their vehicle. . . . The same arguments moved smoothly into main-line religious circles in the United States.[5]

---

5. Otto Scott, "The Conservative Counter-Revolution," *Modern Age* (Summer 1985), pp. 207-8.

Liberation theology appeared as an intellectual force in the early 1970's, and has accelerated. It is the latest in a series of liberal theological movements that the Communists have dominated. This time, they have gained the support of many apostate Roman Catholic priests who never seem to get themselves excommunicated, a sign that the Roman Catholic Church is in deep, deep trouble — the deepest in its history.

The Goal of Liberation

The version of liberation theology that is found in this book is simply an extension to modern times of the Bible's message of salvation and covenantal faithfulness. Biblical liberation begins with *liberation from sin in the life of each God-redeemed (bought-back) individual.* Liberation does not end here, but it must begin here. Without spiritual liberation from Satan and sin, there can be no long-term liberation from political and economic bondage.

Christians should insist in confidence that with widespread liberation from Satan and sin, there will also be liberation from political and economic bondage. Christianity produces good fruit in every area of life. We must not limit the effects of God's healing to the soul of each saved individual. The healing of each redeemed person's soul will spread into every area of the person's life, and from there into society at large. We are *not* talking about some kind of salvation out of this world, as falsely claimed by the Communists. Jesus said:

> I do not pray that You should take them out of the world, but that You should keep them from the evil one. They are not of this world, just as I am not of this world. Sanctify them by Your truth. Your word is truth. As You sent Me into the world, I also have sent them into the world (John 17:15-18).

We are talking about the transformation of this world. Only when the present world has been transformed by the gospel of salvation and the transforming work of the Holy Spirit, as He works through God's redeemed people, will the world at last be delivered completely from sin, at the final judgment (Revelation 20). But first, the kingdoms of this world must be steadily transformed into the kingdom of Christ. In principle, Jesus Christ is now king of all of mankind's kingdoms. He gained this authority by His death and resurrection, His triumph over Satan and sin:

> Then Jesus came and spoke to them, saying, "All authority has been given to Me in heaven and on earth" (Matthew 28:18).

> The kingdoms of this world have become the kingdoms of our Lord and of His Christ, and He shall reign forever and ever (Revelation 11:15).

But it is through the work of His faithful people on earth that this *historical* transfer of kingdom ownership to Christ is to be made manifest in history.

> Go therefore and make disciples of all the nations, baptizing them in the name of the Father and of the Son and of the Holy Spirit, teaching them to observe all things that I have commanded you . . . (Matthew 28:19-20a).

Step by step, person by person, nation by nation, Christians are to *disciple* the nations. This means that they are to bring men under the *discipline* of the legal terms of God's covenant. This happens in history. This is what history is all about. All authority has already been transferred to Christ, in heaven *and* in earth. He has already *in principle* transferred this authority to His people. They are to exercise this God-given authority progressively in history.

> Then comes the end, when He delivers the kingdom to God the Father, when He puts an end to all rule and all authority and power. For He must reign till He has put all enemies under His feet. The last enemy that will be destroyed is death (1 Corinthians 15:24-26).

Christianity Has a Positive Program

There is an old saying in politics: "You can't fight something with nothing." What this world does *not* need is another little book refuting the errors of the Marxist movement known as liberation theology. What this world *does* need is a comprehensive, Bible-based, God-blessed program for building a better world in the here and now, so that Christians will gain the wisdom and experience they need to obey God even better in eternity beyond the grave. Christians need blueprints for social healing.

Let me say right from the beginning that this little book is not a guide for Christians about how to escape responsibilities in this world. God does not call us to abandon earthly responsibilities. He calls us to exercise dominion over every aspect of the earth in His name, to His glory, and by His law:

> Then God said, "Let Us make man in Our image, according to Our likeness; let them have dominion over the fish of the sea, over the birds of the air, and over the cattle, over all the earth and over every creeping thing that creeps on the earth" (Genesis 1:26).

Christians need to understand that their obedience to Christ in history also produces fruit in eternity. Good works bring heavenly rewards from God.

> For no other foundation can anyone lay than that which is laid, which is Jesus Christ. Now if anyone builds on this foundation with gold, silver, precious stones, wood, hay, straw, each one's work will become manifest; for the Day will declare it, because it will be revealed by fire; and the fire will test each one's work, of what sort it is. If anyone's work which he has built on it endures, he will receive a reward. If anyone's work is burned, he will suffer loss; but he himself will be saved, yet so as through fire (1 Corinthians 3:11-15).

There is nothing wrong with wanting rewards in heaven, just so long as we understand that such rewards are the fruit of righteousness done on earth by the grace of God and for the glory of God. We must begin with the desire to please God, not the desire to earn rewards. Paul warns us all that we should fear God,

> who will render to each one according to his deeds: eternal life to those who by patient continuance in doing good seek for glory, honor, and immortality (Romans 2:7).

Every reader should be aware that the Bible is a book about commitment, hard work, faithfulness, and justice *in history*. But it is also a book about two inevitable futures beyond the grave: agony, unrest, and eternal separation from a holy God for those who refuse to accept Jesus Christ as their personal Lord and Savior, as well as rest, rewards, fulfilling work, and eternal communion with the Creator God of the universe for those who do accept Him. The Bible is a book about history, the story of man's creation, rebellion, salvation, and restoration in Christ. It is also a book about the curse of man's environment because of man's sin (Genesis 3:17-19), and about the longing of this cursed creation for deliverance through man's restoration to God through Christ's atoning work on the cross (Romans 8:19-25).

The Bible Is a This-Worldly Book

The Bible is a this-worldly book because it is a book about the Creator God who made this world. The Bible is also an other-worldly book for precisely the same reason: the God who created this world is above and beyond this world, not subject to it, but in full command over it. It is a book about Jesus Christ, the Lord of glory, who was and is over this world, came to earth as both a perfect man and perfect God, died and rose again in the flesh, ascended up to heaven, and will come again in judgment. The Bible is a book about God. Which God? This God:

> He has delivered us from the power of darkness and translated us into the kingdom of the Son of His love, in whom we have redemption through His blood, the forgiveness of sins. He is the image of the invisible God, the firstborn of all creation. For by Him all things were created that are in heaven and that are on earth, visible and invisible, whether thrones or dominions or principalities or powers. All things were created through Him and for Him. And He is before all things, and in Him all things consist. And He is the head of the body, the church, who is the beginning, the firstborn from the dead, that in all things He may have preeminence (Colossians 1:13-18).

This book deals with issues that are universal. It discusses Biblical principles that are valid throughout history and in every culture. It is not to be seen as a well-disguised defense of any particular nation's policies. Nevertheless, no book can escape history. Because we Christians serve the God of history, we cannot pretend that we are not creatures in history. We are people who live and die in particular places and in particular times. Think of yourself. How well could you do your work with the skills you now possess if, somehow, you were miraculously pushed a hundred years into the past or a hundred years into the future? Not very well, I imagine. You are a creature of your time. So am I.

I am a citizen of the United States. But I am also a citizen of a better country, for I am a Christian.

> For our citizenship is in heaven, from which we also eagerly wait for the Savior, the Lord Jesus Christ, who will transform our lowly body that it may be conformed to His glorious body, according to the working by which He is able even to subdue all things to Himself (Philippians 3:20-21).

If you have turned your life over to Jesus Christ, trusting in His work on the cross as your *only* basis of mercy from God on judgment day, then you and I are citizens of the same country in spirit: heaven. In not too many years, you and I will be citizens together in that country in spirit, but without our bodies. We will no longer be earthly participants in history. A Christian must be willing to give up everything except his heavenly "citizenship papers." We must never forget what comes first in this life, for we are recipients of eternal life (John 3:36a).

Christianity was not invented in the United States; it was invented in heaven. The United States is only one of several "authorized distributors" of Christianity, and if its people cease to be faithful, this "distributorship" will pass to others entirely. It should be the goal of every Christian to see to it that he does all that he can to enable his nation to become one of these "distributors." This is what missions are all about. This is also what Christian dominion is all about.

The judgment of God can come upon a nation swiftly. When one nation falls because of apostasy, others must be ready to step in and "stand in the gap." This is also what missions are all about. No nation gets any guarantees from God apart from covenantal faithfulness — obedience to His law through the empowering of the Holy Spirit.

There are those who want people to believe in another gospel, a stolen gospel, a gospel that promises liberation but was invented in the pits of hell, the place of eternal bondage. They are also "distributors" of their religion. Many of these people operate in the United States, exporting this alien religion to the Third World. But the beneficiary of this "export" will not be the United States, nor whatever nations might "import" it. The beneficiaries will be the God-hating, God-denying tyrannical Marxist elite who imitate the Pharaoh of Moses' day, and who also imitate Belshazzar, and Herod, who sought to bring God's church under their bloodstained feet. Whether Cuban-trained or Russian-trained or United States-trained, it makes little difference: they work for a supernatural being, a creature who would tear God from His throne if he could, but since he cannot, he wages war against the church of Jesus Christ.

The war is between heaven and hell. It has been thus from the beginning. It will be thus until Christ returns in final judgment. History has meaning only in terms of this battle. Your nation has meaning, and so does mine, but only in terms of this battle. This battle defines every event, every blade of grass, every birth and death.

The Bible makes it clear: the person who takes his stand against the God of the Bible, and against His eternal standards of right and wrong, will be swept into the ash can, not just of history, but of eternity — an eternal ash can that burns forever, gehenna (hell), which will be dumped into the lake of fire (Revelation 20:14). (It was the Communist "Leon Trotsky" — Lev Bronstein — who coined the phrase, "the ash can of history." His imagery is quite accurate; it was no doubt a heritage of his Judaism, for gehenna was the garbage dump outside of Jerusalem.) The stakes in this "game" (which is not a game) are exceedingly high:

> . . . but there are some who trouble you and want to pervert the gospel of Christ. But even if we, or an angel from heaven, preach any other gospel to you than what we have preached to you, let him be accursed. As we have said before, so now I say again, if anyone preaches any other gospel to you than what you have received, let him be accursed (Galatians 1:7-9).

True Liberation Theology

There is a theology of liberation. It affirms that the God who created all things and who judges all things has also sent His son to die for the sins of mankind. Jesus announced at the beginning of His public ministry:

> The Spirit of the Lord is upon Me, because He has anointed Me to preach the gospel to the poor. He has sent Me to heal the brokenhearted, to preach deliverance to the captives and recovery of sight to the blind, to set at liberty those who are oppressed, to preach the acceptable year of the Lord (Luke 4:18-19).

Christ is the *liberator.* He is the same God who delivered His people out of the bondage of Egypt and the bondage of Medo-Persia. It is the God who raised up Joseph out of an Egyptian prison to become second in command in Egypt, the God who raised up Daniel out of the lions' den to become (again) chief advisor to the Medo-Persian empire. It is the same God who raised up Jesus out of the ultimate prison: death. The Roman Empire became a prison experience for the early church, but then came resurrection: Christians took over the Roman Empire.

There are people in prison and even whole nations in prison. The Soviet Union is the largest prison in mankind's history. No rational person denies that there are prisons in life. Men *are* in desperate need of liberation. But liberation comes through covenantal faithfulness to the God who liberates the righteous, and who will at the day of judgment condemn the unrighteous to spend eternity in a fiery prison. Better to spend time in earthly prisons than in the eternal one. There can be liberation from earthly prisons, for the prison experience has always been a prelude to periods of great dominion for the righteous. There can be no liberation from the eternal prison, and no dominion.

1

CHRIST AND LIBERATION

All things have been delivered to Me by the Father, and no one knows the Son except through the Father. Nor does anyone know the Father except through the Son, and he to whom the Son wills to reveal Him. Come to Me, all you who labor and are heavy laden, and I will give you rest. Take My yoke upon you and learn from Me, for I am gentle and lowly in heart, and you will find rest for your souls. For My yoke is easy and My burden is light (Matthew 11:29-30).

Liberation. The world longs for it. Not just mankind—the whole world:

For I consider that the sufferings of this present time are not worthy to be compared with the glory which shall be revealed in us. For the earnest expectation of the creation eagerly waits for the revealing of the sons of God. For the creation was subject to futility, not willingly, but because of Him who subjected it in hope; because the creation itself also will be delivered from the bondage of corruption into the glorious liberty of the children of God. For we know that the whole creation groans and labors with birth pangs together until now (Romans 8:18-22).

There have been a lot of liberation movements throughout history, but only one has the power to deliver men from bondage: Christianity. God, the Creator of all things, and the Father of the eternal Son, Jesus Christ, delivered all things to Jesus, and He in turn passes these things to those who are chained to Him in love by His law. There is no way to escape tyranny, which is always first the *tyranny of sin*, except through Christ, the liberator.

17

This book is about a war. It's a war between Satan and God. The terms of the battle are good vs. evil. The battlefield is the heart, mind, and soul of man. This is why Jesus quoted Deuteronomy 6:5: "You shall love the Lord your God with all your heart, with all your soul, and with all your mind" (Matthew 22:37). Then He added: "This is the first and great commandment. And the second is like it: You shall love your neighbor as yourself" (22:38-39), citing Leviticus 19:18.

We love God with everything we've got. Then we love our neighbors. How do we show our love for God? By obeying His law. Jesus said: "If you love Me, keep My commandments" (John 14:15).

> Now by this we know that we know Him, if we keep His commandments. He who says, "I know Him," and does not keep His commandments, is a liar, and the truth is not in him. But whoever keeps His word, truly the love of God is perfected in him. By this we know we are in Him. He who says he abides in Him ought himself also to walk just as He walked (1 John 2:3-7).

How do we love our neighbors? The same way we love Jesus Christ: by keeping the law with respect to them. At the end of his section on why we must obey the civil government, Paul writes: "Love does no harm to a neighbor; therefore love is the fulfillment of the law" (Romans 13:10). We obey the law in all our dealings with our neighbors.

Paul says the law that wars against God's law in his mind is a "law of sin," and it leads to captivity to sin (Romans 7:23). How do we gain liberation from this captivity? By faith in Christ's death and bodily resurrection at Calvary.

> But God demonstrates His own love toward us, in that while we were yet sinners, Christ died for us. Much more then, having now been justified by His blood, we shall be saved from wrath through Him. For if when we were enemies we were reconciled to God through the death of His Son, much more, having been reconciled, we shall be saved by His life (Romans 5:8-10).

This is where liberation must begin. All other programs of liberation are fraudulent imitations of this one. The bondage of heart, soul, and mind is where *all* bondage begins. It is bondage to sin. Any other form of liberation has a chain attached to it—a chain leading back to the original tyrant, Satan.

But a chain is inescapable. Man is not autonomous. He does not operate under his own law (*auto* = self; *nomos* = law). He is not self-sufficient. *There is no life without an anchor, and no anchor without a chain.* We serve one of two masters, Jesus said: God or Mammon, meaning the world's principle (Matthew 6:24). Men need to wear the yoke of Christ, which is light (Matthew 11:29-30). For a man to pretend that he needs no yoke and no chain is to throw away the key that unlocks the iron cuffs of sin.

Marx ended the *Communist Manifesto* (1848) with these words: "The proletarians have nothing to lose but their chains. They have a world to win. WORKING MEN OF ALL COUNTRIES, UNITE!" He was wrong, yet his language was correct. Proletarians have nothing to lose but their *chains to sin*; so does everyone else. But to throw off one set of chains in the hope that no one will ever place chains on you again is to believe a lie: it is nothing more than exchanging iron chains for brand-new steel chains, with spikes in them. Each "new, improved" set of chains gets tighter in the history of the progress of sin. Each set gets bloodier.

It is time to proclaim Christ, the liberator of the earth, and Christ the liberator of the nations, for it is Christ, and Christ alone, who liberates the individual from captivity to sin. It is the only liberation worth dying for, because it is the only liberation that gives true life.

The Battlefield

The battlefield has been cosmic. It has involved heaven and earth. But today, it involves mostly the earth. Jesus Christ has come to earth, has lived, died, and has been resurrected *on earth*. The war in heaven is over. Satan no longer confronts God face to face, as he did in the first chapter of the Book of Job. He has been cast out of heaven since the days of Christ.

> And war broke out in heaven: Michael and his angels fought
> against the dragon; and the dragon and his angels fought, but they

did not prevail, nor was a place found for them in heaven any longer. So the great dragon was cast out, that serpent of old, called the Devil and Satan, who deceives the whole world; he was cast to the earth, and his angels were cast with him (Revelation 12:7-9).

We know that this war was in the past, because of the next verses:

> Then I heard a loud voice saying in heaven, "Now salvation, and strength, and the kingdom of our God, and the power of His Christ have come, for the accuser of our brethren, who accused them before our God day and night, has been cast down. And they overcame him by the blood of the lamb and by the word of their testimony. . . ."

The blood of the lamb has been shed. It will not be shed again (Hebrews 9). Thus, we know that Revelation 12 refers to a battle in the past: Calvary.

The ethical battle between God and Satan has been going on at least since the garden of Eden. It was going on when Satan intervened to tempt Job, it was going on during the earthly ministry of Jesus, and it will continue until the final judgment (Revelation 20). There is no permanent peace treaty possible between God and Satan. There can be no permanent peace treaty between their respective followers, either.

The primary arena for today's battle is the earth. This is where Satan concentrates his forces. He tried to attack God by tempting Adam and Eve, and Job, and Jesus Christ in the wilderness (Luke 4). The great arena of this war isn't politics, or economics, or even the church. The great battlefield is the human heart. James writes:

> Where do wars and fights come from among you? Do they not come from your desires for pleasure that war in your members? You lust and do not have. You murder and covet and cannot obtain. You fight and war. You do not have because you do not ask. You ask and do not receive, because you ask amiss, that you may spend it on your pleasures. Adulterers and adulteresses! Do you not know that friendship with the world is enmity with God? Who-

ever therefore wants to be a friend with the world makes himself an enemy of God (James 4:1-4).

How is this battle fought? With manufactured weapons bought with gold and silver? No: "For the weapons of our warfare are not of the flesh but divinely powerful for the destruction of fortresses. We are destroying speculations and every lofty thing raised up against the knowledge of God, and we are taking every thought captive to the obedience of Christ" (1 Corinthians 10:4-5). We are fighting a battle for the mind.

This battle is a war about what kind of law we should observe. It's a battle over *ethics*. Paul writes: "But I see another law in my members, warring against the law of my mind, and bringing me into captivity to the law of sin which is in my members" (Romans 7:23). There was a battle inside him, a war between good and evil. "So then, with the mind I myself serve the law of God, but with the flesh the law of sin" (Romans 7:25b).

Two laws, one man. It is a battle for the *mind*. Whose law will win out, God's or Satan's? Which world is our destiny, the law of freedom or the law of captivity? What is the way to victory? Paul writes: "But now having been set free from sin, and having become slaves of God, you have your fruit to holiness, and the end, everlasting life. For the wages of sin is death, but the gift of God is eternal life in Christ Jesus our Lord" (Romans 6:22-23).

Because this is a battle for the minds of men, it involves every aspect of life. There is no neutrality. Each man has to pick sides. Jesus warned: "He who is not with Me is against Me, and he who does not gather with Me scatters abroad" (Matthew 12:30). Christians often are confused about this. They have been sold a bill of goods by the enemies of God, namely, that there are *zones of neutrality* scattered throughout the creation, and that some sort of common natural law rules these neutral zones. This is a myth. Either God's law rules everything, and promises to bring all things under His righteous judgment, or else God's claim of being God is a lie.

The battle is for the earth. One aspect of this battle is the battle for the nations. The question men need to get answered first and foremost is: "Who's in charge here?" Who is sovereign? And the best way to get this question answered is to find an answer for this one: "Who owns the earth?" The Bible provides one, and only one, definitive answer.

God Owns It All

"In the beginning God created the heavens and the earth" (Genesis 1:1). The Bible begins with the identification of God as the absolute Creator. Since He created the earth, He is the original owner. "The earth is the Lord's, and all it contains, the world and those who dwell in it" (Psalm 24:1). With these words, the Bible asserts God's absolute ownership of everything on earth.

Do you believe these verses? Do you believe any area of life is not owned by God, who is the Creator? Name one. Do you believe that God is someday going to show the whole world that He owns it, at the day of final judgment? If you're a Christian, I'll bet you do. Speaking of Jesus Christ, Paul writes:

> Then comes the end, when He delivers the kingdom to God the Father; when He puts an end to all rule and all authority and power. For He must reign till He has put all enemies under His feet (1 Corinthians 15:24-25).

This is *footstool theology* (Psalm 110:1). It is the basis of our hope in an earthly future dominated by God-fearing, law-abiding, born-again Christian saints.

But answering the question of who owns the earth as the original owner only solves part of the problem. Obviously, God isn't visible on earth. He hasn't set out a bunch of "No Trespassing" signs. He seems to have forfeited ownership (some people argue), or else He has delegated it. How do we know who represents God the owner on earth? We need a *doctrine of representation*.

Establishing the Saints' Claim to the Earth

Why doesn't God seem to own it now? Why are some areas of life seemingly under the exclusive control of Satan, the evil one? *Because Adam sold his birthright to Satan.*

Adam was a man. This means that he was made in God's image (Genesis 1:26). So was Eve. This means that Adam was God's first-born earthly son, the lawful heir to the whole world. God made it for man, and then He placed man over it (Genesis 1:28). *All* of it. It was man's lawful possession, so long as man remained faithful to God.

But Adam sold his birthright to Satan—not for a mess of pottage (a bowl of stew), the way that Esau sold his birthright to Jacob (Genesis 25:29-34). No, Adam sold it for a lie, or at least a half-truth: "You will be like God" (Genesis 3:5). Eve was deceived in this transaction, though disobedient; Adam knew exactly what he was doing (1 Timothy 2:14).

This same lie is the central religious commitment of all forms of humanism, the gospel's ancient rival.

What was God's response? To *disinherit* Adam. He threw Adam and Eve out of the garden. But in grace, He clothed them in animal skins (meaning that some animal was first slain by God). He also gave them extra years of temporal life. But from that day forth, they were *legally disinherited* children. So is every human being at physical birth. Made in God's image, we are born as disinherited children.

Satan has run many things on earth ever since the Fall of man, because Adam defaulted on his assignment. But exactly *how* does Satan run things? *Through his human followers*. Mankind is still mankind, made in God's image. Dominion is still God's assignment to man, not to Satan. God's assignment to man to exercise dominion across the face of the earth is still in force. So Satan has to exercise power through his men. He and his fallen angelic host can scare men, tempt men, confuse men, and even disrupt the decisions of God-hating men, but *they cannot run society directly. God is in charge, waiting for His people to challenge the rulers of the earth and take the steering wheel from them.*

God wants Christians to control the earth on His behalf; Jesus could not have made it more plain than He did when He said:

All authority has been given to Me in heaven and on earth; go therefore and make disciples of all the nations, baptizing them in the name of the Father and of the Son and of the Holy Spirit, teaching them to observe all that I commanded you (Matthew 28:18-20).

Jesus has all power on the earth, and He has all power over nations. It is through the Holy Spirit that He exercises His power. It is His goal that His earthly followers eventually exercise authority over the earth in His name, by His revealed Word, through the power of the Holy Spirit. Satan, unredeemed men, and all ungodly forces want you to stay ignorant of this all-important truth. The church, as the assembly of the saints (saint: he who has access to God's sanctuary in prayer), has political ramifications; because it proclaims governmental wisdom and law for the nations of the earth, it is the "pillar and ground" of truth (1 Timothy 3:15).

Concern for our Father's earth is at the center of Christ's heart. When His disciples asked Him how to pray, He led them into God the Father's perspective:

> Pray, then, in this way: Our Father who art in heaven, Hallowed be Thy name. Thy kingdom come. Thy will be done, On earth as it is in heaven (Matthew 6:9-10, King James Version).

Please notice that the central issue of our praying is to be that God's will be done *on earth*. In similar fashion, when Jesus prayed for His disciples as recorded in John 17:15, He specifically asked not that His disciples be removed from the world, but rather that they be protected from its evils, so that they could be effective in it, discipling it and bringing it under Christ's law.

Losing Ground

The battle for the earth is currently going on, yet most Christians don't know or care. We have been told it doesn't really matter. We have been led to believe that all that God cares about is heaven and the future. Well-meaning Christians have told us this, and evil men have told us this. It has been very effective misinformation, no matter what the source.

Consider the current dimensions of our losses. In the last fifty years, the Moslem religion has increased in size 500%; Hinduism by 117%; Buddhism by 63%, and Christianity by a mere 47%. Not only have we lost two thirds of the globe since 1917 to the Marxists, but we are currently losing the religious populations as well.

It is obvious that Christians are losing ground, figuratively and literally. The question is: What can we do about it? Even more basic is this question: Are we *willing* to do something about resuming our God-ordained position as stewards of the Lord's earth? If you are willing to shoulder that responsibility, then this book is for you. The way to regain the ground we have lost is by becoming knowledgeable and involved in the ordering of earth's governments, including *civil* government.

Immediately, some Christians will bristle at this suggestion. Nevertheless, politics is simply the organized activity of those who are exercising legal and economic power as citizens of the nations.

Since the Lord has given us the task of holding "dominion . . . over all the earth" (Genesis 1:26), we are not taking up our assigned role as stewards if we refuse to become involved in the activities of governing. I further point out: How can we disciple the earth if we are not involved in running it?

Manifesto

Politics is ethical. There are good guys and bad guys, for there is right and wrong. Therefore, any authority or power that man possesses is always ethically held. He serves one of two masters, but he always *serves*. This service is ethical. There is no neutrality.

God is the original and primary owner of the earth, no question about it. But he has *delegated* this ownership to mankind. And the only way Satan could get into power in the first place was by bringing men under him, meaning under him *ethically*. They follow him by disobeying God.

Do you think that Satan could beat God up and take the earth? Hardly. Could he trick an all-knowing God? Did he cheat God in some sort of cosmic card game? Did he sneak in one night and steal it? This is silly, of course, but I'm trying to make a point. We are not talking about God's power vs. Satan's.

Rather, Satan gains earthly power when *people* agree to do his bidding. What is his bidding? *Anything that disobeys God.* He isn't fussy; any old disobedience is fine — or any new disobedience, for that matter. He seeks followers to place under him *ethically.* They submit to him.

In other words, he makes a *covenant* with his people. It is a perverse *reverse* covenant, yet it bears the marks of God's covenant: transcendence ("Ye shall be as God": Genesis 3:5), hierarchy (violating the chain of command: disobedience to God), law (abandoning God's tool of dominion for man), judgment (corrupting God's court system), and extended power over time (rebelliously claiming the inheritance from God). It is a mirror image of the covenant God makes with His people.

This is an important point. *Satan is not creative, for he is not the Creator.* He is a distorter of the truth. He imitates God. Furthermore, man cannot escape God's mark in his very being: the image of God. So man is also an imitator of God, and fallen men are like Satan: they distort and twist the truth. But they are not creative. Thus, even in their sin, they reflect God's standards for man. They cannot escape their creaturehood. They cannot escape their humanity. They remain sons of God, even in hell — disinherited sons.

God truly owns the world. Yet Satan truly has power in this world. What makes the difference between them? How does either God or Satan get visibly into authority in the affairs of this world? *Through their covenanted followers.* God voluntarily delegates considerable authority to men in general, but He specially rewards those who honor Him (1 Samuel 2:30). Satan also delegates part of the power that he possesses, but only for limited purposes. He has no choice in the matter; unlike God, he possesses no original power. Whatever power he possesses comes either directly from God or indirectly from people who have covenanted with him.

Then how is the earth to be liberated from the power of Satan? Only through the renewal of men's characters and the resulting transfer of authority to God's people. But how can this be done? Aren't all men under Satan's power? Didn't we all sin "in Adam"?

How can we get back our birthright?

There is only one way: by submitting to the One who has reclaimed man's birthright, the perfect man Jesus Christ, the only begotten Son of God, who came to earth for a task: *to liberate the earth*. And how did He accomplish this awesome task? By living a life *as a man* in perfect conformity to God's law.

All right, that explains how Jesus Christ reclaimed His inheritance as the *second-born earthly son*. But how does this work itself out in history? Why did this make any difference in history?

Simple: because the inheriting Son died, and rose again. He gained His inheritance by a perfect life, and then He gave it away to His people. He established a new covenant with them. Or, as we also say, He established a new *testament* with them. A testament is a document transferring an inheritance to the lawful heirs. Christians now inherit *through Him*. The rightful heir, Jesus Christ, laid down His life for His friends, demonstrating perfect love. There is no greater love than this (John 15:13).

Satan in principle lost his Adam-given authority the day Christ died. Christians re-inherited it in principle the day Christ rose from the dead.

Summary

We are in a war. This war is a war for the hearts, minds, and souls of men. The issues governing this war are ethical: right vs. wrong. The rival commanders are personal: God vs. Satan. The armies are made up of loyal followers who covenant themselves (*chain* themselves) to one of the two commanders. Every army has a chain of command. There cannot be an army without a chain of command. Each army has a set of rules. Each commander calls his followers to live and die in terms of their assignments. Each commander promises his followers rewards. But only God can promise rewards after physical death. He promises eternal judgment for His enemies.

God promises liberation. So does Satan. One of them is lying. The most momentous intellectual decision that an individual or a civilization can make is this one: to decide which one is lying. The

most momentous public decision a person or a civilization can
make is to choose which army to join. We do not prove our liberation simply by intellect; we prove it *covenantally*: by a public affir-
mation to come under the discipline of the Supreme Allied Commander, Jesus Christ, the Liberator. He is the true anchor. His
chain to that personal anchor is our link to stability and eternal
peace. His chain is His law.

The reasons why it is Christ, and Christ alone, who is the true
liberator of the earth are these:

1. All power has been delivered by God to His Son, Jesus
Christ.
2. Christ calls men to freedom through ethical bondage to
Him.
3. The road to liberation is a moral battlefield: the heart.
4. There is no permanent peace treaty between the commanders.
5. There is no possible peace treaty between the armies.
6. Cease-fires are not peace treaties.
7. The battle is between rival law systems.
8. There is no moral or legal neutrality.
9. God, the Creator, owns the earth.
10. God delegated this ownership to Adam.
11. Adam "sold his birthright" to Satan.
12. Christ reclaimed it at Calvary.
13. Christ delegates ownership to His people.
14. His people are to win back the earth through obedience.
15. Modern Christians have been retreating from responsibility.
16. To get back in the battle for the earth, Christians must re-
affirm the original covenant with God through Christ.

2

THE GOD OF LIBERATION

God spoke all these words, saying: "I am the Lord your God, who brought you out of the land of Egypt, out of the house of bondage. You shall have no other gods before Me" (Exodus 20:1-3).

God announced Himself at Mt. Sinai. It was He who had intervened in history to deliver His people out of bondage. This God is the master of history. The false god of Egypt, Pharaoh, had not survived his confrontation with the God of the Bible. Because there was no god in Egypt powerful enough to call a halt to their liberation, God's people are reminded not to call upon any other god in their worship.

Here is a fundamental point of conflict between Christianity and Marxism. The Marxist does not believe in God. Marx argued that the idea of God stems from the minds of men, which in turn are the product of the mode of production at any point in history. Thus, in Marx's view, a God who actively intervenes in history to deliver His people is a myth.

That was Pharaoh's view, too. "Who is the Lord, that I should obey His voice to let Israel go? I do not know the Lord, nor will I let Israel go" (Exodus 5:2).

We see a statement of this view in the Humanist Manifesto II (1973):

But we can discover no divine purpose or providence for the human species. While there is much that we do not know, humans are responsible for what we are or will become. No deity will save us; we must save ourselves.

29

The Marxist liberation theologians refer to the exodus again and again in their writings. They claim that it is Exodus, above all other books in the Bible, that gives to radical Christians the right of bloody revolution. The exodus of Israel from Egypt is the primary model for Marxism's version of liberation theology.

There is no question that Exodus does provide a model for liberation. Pharaoh was a tyrant. He worshipped foreign gods. In fact, Egyptian theology claimed that the Pharaoh was himself a god, the link between heaven and earth. Thus, Egyptian theology was at bottom *humanism*. God does not tolerate humanism forever. God destroyed Pharaoh and his troops in the Red Sea.

God, Not Revolution, Delivered Israel

There is an important aspect of the exodus story that the liberation theologians just never seem to mention. *The Israelites were never called upon by God to engage in armed revolt against their captors.* God intervened to deliver them, even against the will of their compromising rulers (Exodus 5:20-21). God cut down Egypt in the midst of its glory, but the Israelites had to be hounded out of Egypt. The Egyptians had to beg them to leave, offering them jewels and gold as an incentive (Exodus 12:35-36). As people with a slave mentality, the Israelites preferred to remain in bondage to Egypt rather than to exercise dominion under God. This is why they said to Moses over and over that they wanted to return to Egypt (Numbers 11:5, 18, 20).

The whole message of the Book of Exodus is that God *delivers* His people from bondage, even when they are in partial rebellion to Him. When they are in dedicated obedience to Him, He does not deliver them into bondage in the first place. They exercise dominion over God's enemies under such circumstances (Deuteronomy 28:1-14).

So in no way can the Book of Exodus legitimately be used as a justification for armed revolution. It is true that God will raise up evil, God-hating nations or groups to conduct bloody revolution against the Egyptians of this world. It may be that God is using the Communists to plow up the pagan, power-seeking political systems of the world, in preparation for the triumph of the gospel. But this does not mean that Christians are to aid such revolutionary groups, or praise them, or do anything but challenge them.

When Christians join hands with the Communists to criticize an existing civil government, they are in the process of jumping out of the frying pan into the fire. The tottering power-seeking despots of this world are usually content to let Christians go about their business, just so long as the rulers get their extorted wealth for a while longer. They are not systematic murderers. They are not God-hating atheists intent on stamping out the church. They are just criminals who for a time are in power. They are God's minimal judgments over a rebellious people.

Bring in the Communists, and you get scientific tyranny, self-conscious persecution of the righteous. The Communists are to the dictators what Solomon's son Rehoboam was to Solomon, and what Jeroboam was to Rehoboam. Rehoboam's foolish young counsellors advised him as follows:

> Then the young men who had grown up with him spoke to him, saying, "Thus you should speak to the people who have spoken to you, saying, 'Your father made our yoke heavy, but you make it lighter on us'—thus you shall say to them: 'My little finger shall be thicker than my father's waist! And now, whereas my father laid a heavy yoke on you, I will add to your yoke; my father chastised you with whips, but I will chastise you with scourges!'" (1 Kings 12:10-11).

There was then a revolt against Rehoboam by Jeroboam, who led the ten tribes into a separate nation. But what was the price of this tax rebellion? Idolatry. He made them worship golden calves in order to establish the foundation of a new political kingdom (1 Kings 12:25-33). The Israelites of the Northern Kingdom went out of the frying pan (Rehoboam's high taxes) into the fire (idol worship, and eventually captivity to the Assyrians).

The Russian Experience

In Czarist Russia, just before the revolution, about 20 to 25 million people, or one-third of the white Russian population, were members of a Christian group called the Old Believers. They had been harshly persecuted intermittently by the state church, the Russian Orthodox Church, since the late 1660's. These Old Believers "went underground," hiding their worship activities from the authorities and conducting their religion as they saw fit. They moved as far away from the centers of power as they could. In 1883, the Czar made it illegal for Old Believers to establish their own schools. Education was to be in the hands of the established church, and the religious leaders believed that the children of the Old Believers could be lured away from their parents' religion. Only after the defeat of Russia by the Japanese in 1905 did things improve for the Old Believers. But even in January of 1914, shortly before World War I broke out, the Minister of Education placed restrictions on hiring Old Believers as teachers.

In their resentment against the Czar and the state church, they sometimes participated in the periodic revolts against the Russian State. When the Czarist system began to crumble after 1905, the State had already lost the support of a major segment of its most religiously conservative citizenry. This loss of support helped to produce the Bolshevik revolution, which placed the Old Believers under far greater persecution than the Czar had ever imposed. By retreating from almost all positive social action for centuries, they eventually sealed their doom.

Something similar happened when the Nazis invaded the Ukraine in 1941. The persecution of Ukrainians (in Western Russia) by the Soviets in the 1930's had been horrendous; they had literally been starved to death. It was during these years that Nikita Khrushchev earned his reputation as "butcher of the Ukraine." The Ukrainians at first joined the Nazis by the millions. They hoped for liberation from their Russian Bolshevik masters. But the Nazis imposed another tyranny every bit as bad as Stalin's. What had appeared to be liberation became just another horrible tyranny, with occultism, racism, and socialism as the new religion rather than Bolshevism's atheism and Communism. It does no good to try to leap out of frying pans into fires.

God as Liberator

God announces in the introduction to His Ten Commandments that He had intervened decisively and miraculously in the lives of the Hebrews. This intervention was radically personal. The events of the exodus cannot be cogently explained as a series of impersonal natural events. There could be no doubt in the minds of the Hebrews of Moses' day that God had been the source of their liberation from Egypt. There was certainly no doubt about this in the minds of the people of the Canaanitic city of Jericho, as Rahab informed the spies a generation later (Joshua 2:10-11).

By identifying Himself as the source of their liberation, He announced His total sovereignty over them. A God who intervenes in history is not some distant God. He is a God of power. He possesses the power to reshape nations, seas, and history. No other God has this power; therefore, they are required to worship only Him.

He is also their king. Eastern kings of the second millennium B.C. used a formula for announcing their sovereignty which was similar to this announcement and also similar to God's announcement to Moses of His name (Exodus 6:2). Even when their names were well known, they announced them in the introduction to their proclamation. Then it was customary for him to record his mighty deeds. The Jewish commentator Cassuto summarizes God's announcement: "*I*, the Speaker, am called *YHWH*, and I *am your God* specifically. Although I am the God of the whole earth (xix 5), yet I am also your God in the sense that, in consideration of this sanctification, I have chosen you to be the people of My special possession from among all the peoples of the earth (xix 6); and it is I *who brought you out of the land of Egypt*, not just bringing you forth from one place to another, but liberating you *from the house of bondage*. Hence it behooves you to serve Me not out of fear and dread, in the way that the other peoples are used to worship their gods, but from a sense of love and gratitude."[1]

---

1. U. Cassuto, *A Commentary of the Book of Exodus* (Jerusalem: The Magnes Press, [1951] 1974), p. 241.

He is a God of *power* and of *ethics*. Both of these features of God's being are revealed by His act of freeing the Hebrews from their Egyptian masters. Both love and awe are due to Him. The events of life are controlled by a God who can bring His words to pass.

The Hebrews had this as the historical foundation of their faith in God and His law-order. This law-order is summarized in the Ten Commandments that follow the introduction. The commandments are the foundation of righteous living. The whole of Old Testament law serves as a series of case-law applications of the ten. Thus, they must be regarded as the basis of social institutions and interpersonal relationships. Whatever the area of life under discussion—family, business, charitable association, military command, medicine, etc.—Biblical law governs the actions of men.

Men can choose to ignore the requirements of the law. But God dealt in Egypt and the Red Sea with those who flagrantly and defiantly rejected the rule of His law. The Israelites had experienced firsthand the institutional effects of a social order governed by a law-order different from the Bible's. They had been enslaved. The God who had released them from bondage now announces His standards of righteousness—not just private righteousness but social and institutional righteousness. Thus, the *God of liberation* is simultaneously the *law-giver*. The close association of Biblical law and human freedom is grounded in the very character of God.

The Hebrews could not have misunderstood this relationship between God's law and liberation. God identifies Himself as the deliverer of Israel, and then He sets forth the summary of the law structure that He requires as a standard of human action. *The God of history is the God of ethics.* There can be no Biblical ethics apart from an ultimate standard, yet this standard is fully applicable to history, for the God of history has announced the standard. Ethics must be simultaneously permanent and historically applicable. Permanence must not compromise the applicability of the law in history, and historical circumstances must not relativize the universal standard. The dialectical tension between law and history that undermines every non-Biblical social philosophy is overcome by God, who is the guarantor of His law and the social order that is governed by this law. He is the *guarantor* of the law's permanent applicability because He is the *deliverer*, in time and on earth.

The prophets of Israel repeatedly announced their detailed critiques of Israel and Judah by first recalling that the God in whose name they were coming before the nation was the same God who had delivered them from Egypt (Isaiah 43:3; Jeremiah 6; Hosea 13:4). Having made this identification, they would go on to catalogue the sins of the nation—sins that were prohibited by Biblical law. Ezekiel wrote, citing Leviticus 18:5,

> Therefore I made them go out of the land of Egypt and brought them into the wilderness. And I gave them My statutes and showed them My judgments, "which if a man do, he shall live by them" (Ezekiel 20:10-11).

The New American Standard Version translates this final clause, "if a man observes them, he will live." In other words, the very foundation of life is the law of God, *if* a man lives in terms of this law. The prophets then listed the sins of the nation, which were inevitably bringing death and destruction.

Biblical Law

Can men legitimately have confidence in the law of God in every area of life? Yes. Why is this confidence justified? Because the same God who delivered Israel from the Egyptians also established the laws of every area of life. But this means that the basis of these laws is not man, or random chance, or historical cycles, or the impersonal forces of history, but instead is the *sustaining providence of God.* The guarantor of the reliability of law is a personal Being who delivers His people from those who defy His law.

Biblical law is liberation law for those who have been liberated from sin through God's regenerating grace. Anti-Biblical law is therefore bondage law. Those who proclaim liberation theology but who refuse to be guided by the concrete, explicit revelation of

God concerning economic law are wolves in sheep's clothing. If they are proclaiming some variant of Marxism, socialism, interventionism, or other State-deifying economics, then they are the equivalent of the Egyptians. If they are proclaiming radical anarchism, then they are laying the foundations for an ethical and political backlash which will aid those who are seeking to expand the powers of the State. Men will not live under anarchy; libertinism (sexual and otherwise), which is necessarily a consequence of abolishing all civil laws (anarchism), creates the backlash.

(Historically, the anarchists have allied themselves with Marxist revolutionaries at the beginning of a revolution, but have invariably been destroyed after their former allies capture control of the coercive apparatus of the State. Marx and anarchist Michael Bakunin initially cooperated in the founding of the First International [International Workingmen's Association], the original international Communist revolutionary organization, but the two later split, and Marx and Engels destroyed the organization in the late 1870's — by transferring its headquarters to New York City — rather than allow it to fall into the hands of Bakunin's followers. In the case of the Russian Revolution, the anarchists were among the first dissidents to be arrested by the Cheka, Lenin's secret police.)

The Bible sets forth a true liberation theology, and it undergirds a true liberation society. The specifics of this social and political system are found in God's law. What is commonly called "liberation theology" in the latter decades of the twentieth century is very often warmed-over Marxism, or some sort of socialist economics.

Appeals are made by self-professed liberation theologians to the historic precedent of the exodus, but few if any references are made to the many Old Testament case-law applications of the Ten Commandments. In fact, liberation theologians deny the continuing validity of Old Testament laws that deal with economic relationships; only those laws that *seem* to expand the economic power of the State — and there are very few of these in the Bible — are cited by liberation theologians. This "pick and choose" aspect of modern liberation theology — a choice governed by the standards of socialism and revolution rather than by the standards of orthodox theology—undermines the church's ability to reconstruct social institutions in terms of God's revealed word.

Why, then, have the Bible-believing churches remained silent for so long? Why have they allowed Marxists to steal the idea of liberation and social transformation? One important reason is that the churches are not agreed on the need to offer a positive alternative to humanism. Many churches prefer to hide in the historical shadows until Jesus comes again physically to deliver His people from bondage. They do not believe that God has given us the authority and tools to deliver the world from bondage in His name before He comes again physically. I call this sort of Christianity the escapist religion. (See Chapter Three.)

Summary

Liberation and the law of God go together. God's announcement to His people that He is the God who delivered them from Egypt, and then His presentation of the ten commandments, makes this connection between freedom and Biblical law inescapably clear. To abandon faith in the reliability of God's law is to abandon faith in what the Bible proclaims as the only basis of liberation, namely, liberation under the sovereign power of God, who sustains the universe and calls all men to conform themselves to His ethical standards in every area of life, in time and on earth.

In summary:

1. The Marxist liberation theologians improperly appeal to the example of the exodus.

2. The Israelites did not adopt tactics of armed revolution against the Egyptians.

3. Christians must not work with or aid Marxist, humanist revolutionary movements.

4. The God who liberates is the God who controls history.

5. This God is the God of power and ethics.

6. God has given His people His law in order to liberate them from sin in every area of life.

7. God has given His people His law in order to enable them to exercise dominion in every area of life.

8. God's laws are laws of life for redeemed men.

9. Biblical law is liberation law for sin-liberated people.

10. Anything against God's law results in bondage.

11. Liberation and the law of God go together.

12. Most churches have not preached this truth.

13. Marxists and humanists have stolen the language and vision of the Bible.

3

THE ENEMIES OF LIBERATION

"No man can serve two masters; for either he will hate the one
and love the other, or else he will be loyal to the one and despise the
other. You cannot serve God and mammon" (Matthew 6:24).

Bondage is an inescapable concept. It is never a question of
"bondage vs. no bondage." It is always a question of *bondage to whom*.
Jesus warned against serving mammon. What was mammon?
Was it money? Yes. Was it power? Yes. Was it anything in the
heart of man that man raises up above God? Yes. Jesus was simply repeating the challenge that the prophet Elijah had made to
the people of Israel almost 800 years earlier.

And Elijah came to all the people, and said, "How long will you
falter between two opinions? If the Lord is God, follow Him; but if
Baal, then follow him." But the people answered him not a word
(1 Kings 18:21).

The people were trying to "play it safe." They were unwilling
to choose God on the basis of God's word, or even on the basis of
all the miracles God had shown them when He delivered their
ancestors from Egypt 700 years earlier. No, they wanted to see
which sacrificial animals the fire would consume, Elijah's or the
false prophets'. They wanted a sign from God. They worshipped
power, so they wanted a sign of power.

Worshipping Power

That is the same challenge today: worship God or worship
power. Not that God doesn't have power. He has total power. But
He wants men to worship Him because He is righteous, not sim-

ply because He has power. Satan, in contrast, wants men to worship power rather than God, for he has no righteousness, but he does have limited though highly concentrated power. For brief periods in history, Satan's visible power is greater than the visible power possessed by God's people. During times of apostasy and rebellion, God removes power from His people. So Satan calls men to think about power, fret about power, and seek power. Jesus understood this weakness in the hearts of men, and He warned:

> "But seek first the kingdom of God and His righteousness, and all these things shall be added unto you" (Matthew 6:33).

Jesus warned about something else, too:

> "Whatever I tell you in the dark, speak in the light; and what you hear in the ear, preach on the housetops. And do not fear those who kill the body but cannot kill the soul. But rather fear Him who is able to destroy both soul and body in hell" (Matthew 10:27-28).

The Satanists worship power, but they have no power over men beyond the grave. Therefore, they must concentrate whatever limited power they possess in history. They do everything they can to focus men's eyes on earthly power. They want to scare us to death with their power.

What is the proper response by Christians? To take power seriously, but not to worship it. To understand that Christians have access to the very throne of God in prayer. Christians can appeal to the God who possesses total power. They can do this in private prayer, and they can do it in public worship (see Psalm 83 for an example of such a public prayer). Christians worship God, not mammon. They worship the one who can destroy both body and soul in hell, not simply mammon, who can at best destroy only the body in history. And to do even this much, Satan must first get God's permission (Job 1).

Is it moral for Christians to seek power? If not, why not? If so, under what conditions is it moral? This has been an ancient debate in the history of Christianity.

Three Religious Worldviews

There are three major outlooks regarding power that prevail today. Two of them oppose liberation; one favors it. Of the two systems that oppose it, one comes in the name of power, and the other in the name of escaping power. These religious worldviews are ancient rivals. They have been at war with each other, yet making temporary alliances with each other, as far back as we have historical records. I call them the power religion, the escapist religion, and the dominion religion.

Consider the Hebrew slaves in Egypt. They wanted an escape from bondage, for they groaned. God heard their groaning (Exodus 2:24; 6:5). Yet when He sent Moses and Aaron to deliver them, what was the response of the rulers of Israel? To try to get Moses to stop confronting Pharaoh.

> Then, as they came out from Pharaoh, they met Moses and Aaron who stood there to meet them. And they said to them, "Let the LORD look on you and judge, because you have made us abhorrent in the sight of Pharaoh and in the sight of his servants, to put a sword in their hand to kill us" (Exodus 5:20-21).

They feared the sword of Pharaoh more than they feared bondage to Pharaoh. But this also meant that they feared the gods of Egypt more than they feared the God of Abraham, Isaac, and Jacob. So God had to demonstrate His power over the gods of Egypt with the ten plagues. Still, the Israelites feared Pharaoh. So God delivered them from Pharaoh and drowned the Egyptians in the sea. Then they started fearing the far weaker Canaanites. They lived in terms of fear because they worshipped power more than they worshipped God. They wanted escape from their God-given responsibilities, and this meant worshipping the power of Satan's kingdoms. Their escapist religion made them allies of Satan's power religion.

The history of man can be understood in terms of the increasing religious self-consciousness of man. Therefore, in our day these two issues — power vs. escape — have become sharper and less easily deferred. We need to consider the three viewpoints in detail.

1. *Power Religion*

This is a religious viewpoint which affirms that the most important goal for a man, group, or species, is the capture and maintenance of power. Power is seen as the chief attribute of God, or if the religion is officially atheistic, then the chief attribute of man. This perspective is a satanic perversion of God's command to man to exercise dominion over all the creation (Gen. 1:26-28).[1] It is the attempt to exercise dominion apart from covenantal subordination to the true Creator God.

What distinguishes Biblical *dominion religion* from satanic *power religion* is ethics. Is the person who seeks power doing so for the glory of God, and for himself secondarily, and only to the extent that he is God's lawful and covenantally faithful representative? If so, he will act in terms of God's ethical standards and in terms of a profession of faith in God. The church has recognized this two-fold requirement historically, and has established a dual requirement for membership: profession of faith and a godly life.

In contrast, power religion is a religion of *autonomy.* It affirms that "My power and the might of my hand have gained me this wealth" (Deuteronomy 8:17). It seeks power or wealth in order to make credible this very claim.

Wealth and power are aspects of both religions. Wealth and power are covenantal manifestations of the success of rival religious views. This is why God warns His people not to believe that their autonomous actions gained them their blessings: "And you shall remember the Lord your God: for it is He who gives you power to get wealth, that He may establish His covenant which He swore to your fathers, as it is this day" (Deuteronomy 8:18). It must be recognized that God's opponents also want visible confirmation of the validity of their covenant with death, but God warns them that "the wealth of the sinner is stored up for the righteous" (Proverbs 13:22b). The entry of the Hebrews into Canaan was supposed to remind them of this fact: the Canaanites had

---

1. Gary North, *The Dominion Covenant: Genesis* (Tyler, Texas: Institute for Christian Economics, 1982).

built homes and vineyards to no avail; their enemies, the Hebrews, inherited them (Joshua 24:13).

Those who believe in power religion have refused to see that long-term wealth in any society is the product of ethical conformity to God's law. They have sought the blessings of God's covenant while denying the validity and eternally binding ethical standards of that covenant. In short, they have confused the fruits of Christianity with the roots. They have attempted to chop away the roots but preserve the fruits.

2. Escapist Religion

This is the second great tradition of antichristian religion. Seeing that the exercise of autonomous power is a snare and a delusion, the proponents of escapist religion have sought to insulate themselves from the general culture—a culture maintained by power. They have fled the responsibilities of worldwide dominion, or even regional dominion, in the hope that God will excuse them from the general dominion covenant.

The Christian version of the escapist religion is sometimes called "pietism," but its theological roots can be traced back to the ancient heresy of *mysticism*. Rather than proclaiming the requirement of *ethical union* with Jesus Christ, the perfect man, the mystic calls for *metaphysical union* with a monistic, unified god. In the early church, there were many types of mysticism, but the most feared rival religion which continually infiltrated the church was *gnosticism*. It proclaimed many doctrines, but the essence of gnostic faith was radical individualism: retreat from the material realm and escape to a higher, purer, spiritual realm through techniques of self-manipulation—asceticism, higher consciousness, and initiation into secret mysteries. Gnosticism survives as a way of thinking and acting (or failing to act) even today. The essence of this faith is its *antinomianism*—anti (against) nomos (law). Gnostics despise the law of God. But their hatred for the law of God leads them to accept the laws of the State. To escape from God's law, they accept humanism's law.

The basic idea lying behind escapist religion is the denial of the dominion covenant. The escape religionist believes that the techniques of self-discipline, whether under God or apart from God (Buddhism), offer power over only limited areas of life. They attempt to conserve their power by focusing their ethical concern on progressively (regressively) narrower areas of personal responsibility. The "true believer" thinks that he will gain more control over himself and his narrow environment by restricting his self-imposed zones of responsibility. His concern is self, from start to finish; his attempt to escape from responsibilities beyond the narrow confines of self is a program for gaining power over self. It is a religion of works, of *self-salvation*. A man "humbles" himself—admits that there are limits to his power, and therefore limits to the range of his responsibilities—only to elevate self to a position of hypothetically God-like spirituality.

Escapist religion proclaims institutional peace—"peace at any price." Ezekiel responded to such an assertion in the name of God: ". . . they have seduced My people, saying, 'Peace!' when there is no peace" (Ezekiel 13:10a). Patrick Henry's inflammatory words were taken from Jeremiah: "They have also healed the hurt of My people slightly, saying, 'Peace, peace!' when there is no peace" (Jeremiah 6:14). This rival religion proclaims peace because it has little interest in the systematic efforts that are always required to purify institutions as a prelude to social reconstruction.

In short, escapist religion calls for flight from the world. Its advocates may hide their real concern—the systematic abandonment of a world supposedly so corrupt that nothing can be done to overcome widespread cultural evil—by appealing to their moral responsibility of "sharing Christ to the world" or "building up the Church" rather than rebuilding civilization, but their ultimate concern is *personal flight from responsibility*. Rushdoony calls this the revolt against maturity.

3. Dominion Religion

This is the orthodox faith. It proclaims the sovereignty of God, the reliability of the historic creeds, the necessity of standing up for principle, and the requirement that faithful men take risks for God's sake. It proclaims that through the exercise of saving faith, and through ethical conformity to God's revealed law, regenerate men will increase the extent of their dominion over the earth. It is a religion of conquest — *conquest through ethics*. The goal is ethical conformity to God, but the results of this conformity involve dominion — over lawful subordinates, over ethical rebels, and over nature. This is the message of Deuteronomy 28:1-14. It is also the message of Jesus Christ, who walked perfectly in God's statutes and in God's Spirit, and who then was granted total power over all creation by the Father (Matthew 28:18). I am not speaking here of the pre-Incarnate Second Person of the Trinity, who always had total power; I am speaking of the Incarnated Christ, the perfect man, who *gained* total power through ethical conformity to God and through His death and resurrection.

Dominion religion recognizes the relationship between *righteousness* and *authority*, between covenantal faithfulness and covenantal blessings. Those who are faithful in little things are given greater authority. This is the meaning of Christ's parable of the talents (Matthew 26:14-30). The process of progressive dominion is a function of *progressive moral sanctification*, both personal-individual and institutional (family, church, business, school, civil government, etc.).

Covenantal religion is always *openly, forthrightly creedal;* it has a public theology. Power religion and escapist religion may or may not be openly creedal. Nevertheless, every worldview has a creed, even if that permanent creed states that "there is no permanent creed." *Creeds are inescapable concepts.* It is never a question of "creed vs. no creed"; it is a question of *which* creed.

We must understand, however, that power religion seldom announces itself as an inescapably creedal religion, although Communism and Nazism have been exceptions to this general rule. In the setting of the "liberal" West, power religion's advocates seldom announce their intentions openly until the final phases of their capture of institutional power.

Historically, Christianity has been divided between dominion religionists and escape religionists. For example, European pietists — the Mennonites and Amish — have been characterized by their withdrawal from politics and culture. These two groups have also been pacifists. Today's Christian escapists (pietistic fundamentalists) want only to defer the power vs. escape confrontation, until Jesus comes back again and solves society's problems by means of His power. This theology of deferred social responsibility has become visibly bankrupt in the 1980's.

Miranda's Challenge

The Marxist liberation theologians recognize this escapist impulse in popular Christianity. They ridicule Christianity by arguing that this escape religion is the essence of Christianity, the only alternative to revolutionary socialism. This is a false choice. The Marxists ignore dominion theology. They pretend that this alternative does not exist and has never existed. But it does exist.

The Marxist liberation theologian José Miranda preaches common ownership of all goods. He challenges Christians who defend the present non-Communist social order. They are all escapists, he says. They are all defenders of a socially irrelevant and historically impotent faith. He is self-conscious about the ineffectiveness of escapist Christianity:

> Now, the Matthean expression "the kingdom of the heavens" was the only one serving the escapist theologians as pretext for maintaining that the kingdom was to be realized in the other world. Not even texts about glory or entering into glory provided them any support, for the Psalms explicitly teach, "Salvation surrounds those who fear him, so that the glory will dwell in our land" (Psalm 85:10).[2]

> Hence what paradise might be, or being with Christ, or Abraham's bosom, or the heavenly treasure, is a question we could well leave aside, because what matters to us is the definitive kingdom, which constitutes the central content of the message of Jesus. The escapists can have paradise.[3]

---

2. José Miranda, *Communism in the Bible* (Maryknoll, New York: Orbis Books, 1982), p. 14.

3. *Ibid.*, p. 15.

To speak of a kingdom of God in the other world is not only to found a new religion without any relationship with the teaching of Christ (for none of the texts wielded by escapist theology mentions the kingdom); it is to assert exactly the contrary of what Christ teaches: "The kingdom has come unto you," and "Your kingdom come." The fact that tradition has taught for centuries that the kingdom is in the other world only demonstrates that that tradition betrayed Jesus and founded another religion entirely different.[4]

The enormous appeal of liberation theology in Latin America (and on seminary campuses in the United States) stems from its ability to transfer powerful concepts of the Bible to the revolutionary Marxist vision. Miranda is correct about the other-worldly emphasis of the escapist fundamentalist and traditional religion. He is incorrect about the supposed communism of the gospel. But it takes a degree of theological sophistication uncommon in Christian circles to pinpoint his errors and overcome them by an appeal to the Bible, without also destroying the foundation of the escapist versions of Christianity. Thus, the challenge of liberation theology goes unanswered by those who have the best alternative in their hands (the Bible) but who do not understand what it says about the kingdom of God on earth and in history.

The power religion in our day is humanistic elitism (including Communism), which has as its goal autonomous man's conquest of nature (including mankind). It often misuses the intellectual discipline of science in this effort. It is opposed by the escapist religion, as well as by the ethics-based dominion religion. Implicitly, both rivals to Christianity are opposed to the idea that legitimate long-term progress is possible prior to the coming of Christ in power. The Bible offers as an alternative a dominion concept of long-term scientific, economic, and intellectual progress which can overcome most (though not all) of the limits placed by God on His creation as a part of His curse.

Ethics and Deliverance

We are to take Christ's yoke on us. We are to make a covenant with God. The God who delivered the Hebrews from the bondage

---

4. *Ibid.*, p. 17.

to Egypt and Egypt's gods also offers men deliverance today. But this deliverance is always *covenantal*. It is in terms of a covenant. It is not a lawless covenant; it is a lawful covenant. Christ calls us to be bondservants to Him.

Are we to seek political and freedom? Of course. Free men are responsible men. They have more opportunities to serve God. Paul tells us this:

> Let each one remain in the same calling in which he was called. Were you called while a slave? Do not be concerned about it; but if you can be made free, rather use it. For he who is called in the Lord while a slave is the Lord's freedman. Likewise he who is called while free is Christ's slave. You were bought at a price; do not become the slaves of men (1 Corinthians 7:20-23).

Are we to complain to God because we do not have some sort of total freedom, some promised *autonomy* (self-law). No, for that is the way of bondage to Satan, sin, and political servitude. That is how we become the slaves of men. That is what we are to avoid becoming. We are to seek to conform ourselves ethically to God; then freedom shall be added unto us. We are to seek *first things first*.

Summary

Those who tell men that God, Communism, humanism, or any other source of authority can liberate men from all responsibility to any and all institutions are preaching a false religion. Marx's dream of the withering away of the state has led to the nightmare of the totalitarian Communist state. Men must serve God or some authority other than God. Man is made to serve. But he is also made to exercise dominion. He is to serve God and exercise dominion. He is to be subordinate to God but sovereign as God's steward over the creation. Any movement that successfully tempts men to make themselves subordinate to anything else than the God of the Bible inevitably leads its followers into sin and therefore into tyranny.

We must choose whom we will serve; Baal or God, Mammon

or God. The debate between the Bible's liberation theology and Marxism's liberation theology centers on this choice.

In summary:

1. Bondage is an inescapable concept.

2. It is always the question: "To whom will I be bound?"

3. Those who worship power worship Satan, who has less power than God.

4. We are warned to fear Him who can destroy the body and the soul in eternal judgment.

5. There are three religious worldviews: power religion, escapist religion, and Biblical dominion religion.

6. Power religion is a religion of autonomy: self-made law apart from God.

7. Escapist religion is a religion of antinomianism: denying the power of God's law.

8. It is also a religion of self-salvation: asceticism unto salvation.

9. Dominion religion is ethical religion that affirms the power of God's law: conquest through ethics.

10. The dominion religion affirms the reality of time.

11. Dominion is through progressive moral sanctification: personal and institutional.

12. Dominion religion is creedal: fixed principles.

13. The Marxist liberation theologians assume that their power religion is the only alternative to pietism's escapist religion.

14. Christ's yoke delivers us.

15. It is a *covenantal* yoke.

16. It involves adherence by grace to Biblical law.

17. Autonomy (self-made law) is the road to bondage under Satan.

4

THE COVENANT OF LIBERATION

And you shall remember the LORD your God, for it is He who gives you power to get wealth, that He may establish His covenant which He swore to your fathers, as it is this day. Then shall it be, if you by any means forget the LORD your God, and follow other gods, and serve them and worship them, I testify against you this day that you shall surely perish. As the nations which the LORD destroys before you, so shall you perish, because you would not be obedient to the voice of the LORD your God (Deuteronomy 8:18-20).

Biblical religion is covenantal religion. Like bondage, the covenant is an inescapable concept. It is never a question of "covenant vs. no covenant." It is always a question of *whose* covenant.

The Bible teaches that there are four covenants: personal, familial, ecclesiastical, and civil. Each is marked by what theologians call a *self-maledictory oath*. Such an oath calls God's wrath down on the swearer if he disobeys the covenant. God Himself established a covenant with Abraham, cutting animals in pieces and moving in between them. This signified God's assurance that He would be faithful to the terms of His covenant with Abraham, and with such complete faithfulness that if He violated the covenant, He would be torn to pieces, like the animals (Genesis 15:7-21).

An individual does not generally make such a covenant directly before God, except when he makes a vow to God (Numbers 30), but Adam implicitly made such a vow when God placed him under the covenant of life. He was not to eat of the tree of the knowledge of good and evil. He did eat, broke the vow, and placed all his heirs under this same vow. The wrath of God is on us all, unless we accept God's substitute, Jesus Christ, who called down the wrath of God on Himself.

Other institutions are contractual or fellowship institutions, not covenantal. Only three institutions possess the God-ordained right to impose binding oaths before God: family, church, and state. This is why self-maledictory oaths taken to secret societies are unbiblical. They are Satan's attempt to establish non-Biblical covenants.

Without *bonding*—meaning personal and judicial bonding—to God by means of a lawful covenant, neither the individual nor a society can sustain long-term dominion. This is why we need to understand true covenants and false ones. When we understand the covenants, we can better understand the nature of the ethical war we are in.

Pastor Ray Sutton argues persuasively in his book on the covenant, *That You May Prosper* (1987) that there is a five-part structure to both the Old Testament and New Testament covenant model. Professor Meredith Kline discovered a five-point structure in the Book of Deuteronomy, although it differs somewhat from Sutton's model, but he did not pursue its implications. Sutton does pursue them. Here is the basic outline of the covenant throughout the Bible:

1. Transcendence/Immanence (presence)
2. Hierarchy/Authority (submission)
3. Law/Dominion (stipulations)
4. Judgment/Oath (sanctions)
5. Inheritance/Continuity (survival)

The language may seem a bit technical. We can put the words differently and make things more practical:

1. Who's in charge here?
2. To whom do I report?
3. What are my orders?
4. What do I get if I obey (disobey)?
5. Does this outfit have a future?

This may not seem to be a revolutionary insight, but it is. It is not possible for me to reproduce here all of his arguments that favor this interpretation, nor discuss all of its applications. Still, I need to survey this outline, and then compare it with Satan's version, for Satan also uses a very similar covenant structure.

The Covenant's Structure

Both Kline and Sutton argue that this same structure is found in the suzerainty treaties of the ancient world. The king (suzerain) would initially announce his sovereignty over a nation, demand loyalty, impose sanctions for disobedience, offer protection for obedience, publish a law code, and establish the rules of succession. Sutton believes that these treaties were simply imitations of a fundamental structure of human government which is inherent in man's relationship with God.

1. Transcendence/Immanence (presence)

The heresy of deism argues that God is so far above His creation that He has no personal contact with it. He started it, almost as a watchmaker winds up a clock, but then He no longer interferes with it. God becomes wholly impersonal to His creation in history.

The heresy of pantheism argues that God is identical with His creation, and is immersed in it. He cannot control it because He is bound to it. He is not sovereign over it. This god, too, is impersonal.

The Bible rejects both views: total impersonal transcendence and total impersonal immanence.

Biblical Transcendence

God is the Creator. He is therefore above His creation and radically different from it. He shares no common being with it. In Genesis 1:1 we read, "In the beginning God created the heavens and the earth." He is the Creator God. He is not part of the Creation. Thus, the Bible announces the *Creator/creature distinction*. This distinction is fundamental to every aspect of life. God is not to be in any way confused with His creation. He is not part of a hypothetical "chain of being" with His creation. As the Psalmist put it:

For You, LORD, are most high above all the earth: you are exalted far above all gods (Psalm 97:9).

The LORD is great in Zion; and He is high above all the peoples (Psalm 99:2).

Perhaps the crucial verses in the Bible that deal with God's transcendence are Isaiah 55:8-9:

For My thoughts are not your thoughts, nor are your ways My ways, says the LORD. For as the heavens are higher than the earth, so are My ways higher than your ways, and My thoughts than your thoughts.

Those who are familiar with the writings of Christian philosopher Cornelius Van Til will recognize that the Creator/creature distinction is Van Til's starting point: the *sovereignty of God* and therefore the *non-autonomy of man*. Van Til has offered an approach to apologetics (the intellectual defense of the faith) that begins and ends with God and God's revelation of Himself in the Bible. We are supposed to begin all our thoughts with the idea that the God of the Bible is in control of everything. We know that all unbelievers (anti-Christians) resist this intellectual requirement.

This is a very important difference between the two types of liberation theology. The Biblical version insists that men bring all their thoughts captive under Christ, under the Bible. The Marxist version insists on bringing mankind under the supposed "impersonal forces of dialectical history."

Biblical Presence

But God is not simply above man in terms of His being. He is close to man in terms of His presence. God is present everywhere in the creation. He is *omnipresent*. He is *immanent*, not just transcendent. Solomon announced:

But will God indeed dwell on the earth? Behold, heaven and the heaven of heavens cannot contain You. How much less the temple which I have built! (1 Kings 8:27).

Even more powerful is Psalm 139:7-9:

> Where can I go from Your Spirit? Or where can I flee from Your presence? If I ascend into heaven, You are there. If I make my bed in hell, behold, You are there. If I take the wings of the morning, and dwell in the uttermost parts of the sea, even there Your hand shall lead me, and Your right hand shall hold me.

Near and far, high and low, in heaven and in hell, God is present with His creation.

> "Am I a God near at hand," says the LORD, "And not a God afar off? Can anyone hide himself in secret places, so I shall not see him?" says the LORD. "Do I not fill heaven and earth?" says the LORD (Jeremiah 23:23-24).

This is a crucial aspect of God's covenant. It is the one that Satan, a creature, does not possess. Satan is not omnipresent; he is neither transcendent nor immanent. This is why Satan needs (and never gets) followers who fully understand his will and perfectly obey it. This is why the crucial aspect of Satan's covenant is hierarchy, which is section two of God's covenant.

2. Hierarchy/Authority (submission)

The second principle of the covenant is that of hierarchy/authority. The King of creation comes before men and demands that they submit to Him. God required Adam to obey Him. The relationship between God and man is therefore one of *command and obedience*. The covenant is therefore a *bond*. It is a *personal* relationship between responsible individuals. It is to be a *union*. But this union is not ontological. It is not a union of common "being." God is not some pantheistic being. Men are not evolving into God (Eastern religion). The covenant establishes a personal relationship based on *authority and submission*.

Each person is wholly responsible before God. God needs no intermediary institution to command a person. No person stands before God on judgment day with a committee of sinners beside him who will take some of the blame. Thus, God constructs a *bottom-up* hierarchy. He deals with each person individually. Social institutions therefore must not usurp God's function as sovereign

Creator and Sustainer. Men are to make their own mistakes and successes. Each man is to work out his salvation (or damnation) in fear and trembling (Philippians 2:12). Other men are to sit in judgment over him only when he commits public evil. They are not to command him as imitation gods. They are not to issue comprehensive commands and monitor him constantly. That is God's job, not man's.

Thus, God's hierarchy produces social freedom. It relieves mankind from any pretended autonomy from God's total sovereignty. Men are not to seek to create predestinating hierarchies. They can leave their fellow men alone, so long as God's institutional laws are obeyed in public.

3. Law/Dominion (stipulations)

The third aspect of the covenant is its *ethical* quality. The terms of submission are ethical. The union between covenant-keepers and their God is an ethical union. The disunion between covenant-breakers and God is equally ethical: they are rebels against His law. Adam's fall into sin did not take place because he lacked some essence, some aspect of "being." He was created perfect. He fell willfully. He knew exactly what he was doing. "Adam was not deceived," Paul writes (1 Timothy 2:14a).

This emphasis on ethics separates Biblical religion from pagan religion. Man is supposed to exercise dominion, but not autonomous power. He is not to seek power through magic, or through any attempted manipulation of God or the universe. Dominion is based on adherence to the law of God—by Christ, perfectly and definitively, and by men, subordinately and progressively. Thus, ethics is set in opposition to magic.

4. Judgment/Oath (sanctions)

The fourth aspect of the covenant is its judicial character. The essence of maturity is man's ability to render God-honoring judgment. God renders definitive judgment; man is to render analogous judgment—judging events as God's creatures, yet always with God's standards (laws) in mind.

During the creation week, God said "It is good" after each day. He *evaluated* His own work, and He *rendered judgment verbally.* God is the supreme King, but also the supreme Judge. When He *declares* a man innocent, because of His grace to the person through the gift of saving faith, God thereby imputes Christ's righteousness to him. Without God's declaration of salvation, meaning without the imputation of Christ's righteousness to overcome the imputation of Adam's sin, there is no salvation.

When a covenant is "cut," men are reminded of both the blessings and the cursings attached to the covenant. There are oaths and vows. There are covenant rituals. There are visible signs and seals. We see this in the church (baptism, Lord's Supper), the family (marriage ceremony), and in civil government (oath-taking of civil officers).

5. Inheritance/Continuity (survival)

Finally, there is the legitimacy/inheritance aspect of the covenant. There are covenantally specified standards that govern the transfer of the blessings of God to the next generation. In other words, the covenant extends over time and across generations. *The covenant is a bond which links past, present, and future.* It has implications for men's time perspectives. It makes covenantally faithful people mindful of the earthly future after they die. It also makes them respectful of the past. For example, they assume that the terms of the covenant do not change in principle. At the same time, they also know that they must be diligent in seeking to apply the fixed ethical terms of the covenant to new historical situations. They are respectful of great historic creeds, and they are also advocates of progress, creedal and otherwise. They believe in change *within the fixed ethical terms of the covenant.*

Adam was disinherited by God because of his sin. The second Adam, Jesus Christ, has re-established this forfeited inheritance, and it is now passed to those adopted into God's family through the grace of God (John 1:12). "The wealth of the sinner is stored up for the righteous" (Proverbs 13:22a).

Satan's Imitation Covenant

When Adam and Eve ate the forbidden fruit, they were eating a communion meal with the devil. This is what Paul says that we must not do as Christians (1 Corinthians 10). To eat a meal with a person's god, the person must be under a covenant. This is why in many pagan societies, or in satanist cults in Christian societies, pacts are made between the local demon (or Satan) and the members of the cult.

Let us examine Satan's covenant structure:

1. Transcendence/Immanence (presence)
2. Hierarchy/Authority (submission)
3. Anti-Ethics/pro-magic (manipulation)
4. Judgment/Oath (sanctions)
5. Inheritance/Continuity (survival)

Not surprisingly, it is very similar to God's covenant.

1. Transcendence/Immanence (presence)

The first point is a lie. Satan possesses power, though less power than he possessed before the death, resurrection, and ascension of Jesus Christ, and the sending of the Holy Spirit at Pentecost. Satan has never been God. He has never possessed omnipotence, omniscience, and omnipresence. He possesses *delegated* power for limited purposes (Job 1). He knows a great deal, but he does not know everything. Since Calvary, his head has been crushed in principle (Genesis 3:15). He is a creature; he cannot be everywhere at once.

The saints of God have instant access to God through prayer. That is what the meaning of "saint" is: the person who has access to the *sanctuary*. Jesus sits at God's right hand; the Holy Spirit utters prayers for us. Satan's followers have nothing comparable to this sort of universal direct access to their god, because Satan can be in only one place at a time.

2. Hierarchy/Authority (submission)

Because point one is a lie, Satan must rely heavily on his system of hierarchy. Subordinate demons provide him with information. Presumably, so do subordinate humans. Satan needs a chain of command in a way that God does not. God uses a chain of command in history, but He does not need one. He is not dependent on man or angels to exercise His power, knowledge, and authority.

The problem facing Satan is that he needs the chain of command. It needs to function as an alternative to God's perfect power and knowledge. To imitate the omnipotence and omniscience of God, *Satan must impose the threat of judgment.* He is a creature, yet to maintain his kingdom, he needs the power of God. Thus, he must selectively impose power—not all at once and everywhere, but as best he can, sometimes directly but usually at a distance through his followers. No principle of restraint is supposed to stand in his way.

Thus, Satan's kingdom is a top-down kingdom. It is a kingdom of tyranny by its very nature.

Common to Communist regimes is a system of street informants, apartment informants, and even child informants. Every word and action of every citizen is supposed to be monitored, to see to it that everyone conforms to the latest Communist Party line. Why all this control? Because Satan trusts no one under him. He is a rebel; his subordinates are also rebellious. He knows their motivations.

He needs total information. Everyone is pressured to inform on everyone else. No one can trust anyone else. This reduces everyone to a condition of a slave. Each person is dependent on what his superiors tell him, yet he is at the mercy of lying subordinates. Lying becomes a way of life; it is perhaps the chief form of rebellion in the society of Satan. By lying, people try to escape control. The whole system, top to bottom, and bottom back to top, is based on deception. Satan is a liar; he builds a kingdom of lies.

3. *Anti-Ethics/pro-magic (manipulation)*

Satan seeks power above all. So do his followers. To gain power, they need to violate God's law. They cannot do this perfectly. God restrains them. Furthermore, any creature that denies all law cannot exercise power. Try to run an army or a revolution without a chain of command; it is impossible. But a chain of command requires law of some kind. For example, Stalin in the late 1930's purged the top officers of the Red Army. This weakened the army so badly that Hitler's forces very nearly defeated the Soviet Army in the second half of 1941.

Satan acknowledges no fixed principles, for fixed principles point to God. Satan is the original evolutionist. He has always sought power unrestricted by law. All humanist systems preach relativism. There are no fixed moral laws, or any other laws. Law changes with circumstances, the humanist says.

What Satan offers in place of law is magic. His people try to gain power, not by obedience to God's ethical laws, but rather by magical manipulation or political tyranny. They use formulas, incantations, or other rituals. They manipulate people by adopting demonic symbols. They reject the Biblical covenant's third point, permanent ethics.

4. Judgment/Oath (sanctions)

The Bible says that the church will judge the angels (1 Corinthians 6:3). Satan resents this. Thus, he seeks to impose earthly judgment before the final judgment. He seeks to imitate God. God rewards some and sends others to hell. Satan imitates this.

Satanic governments invariably impose torture. They set up large numbers of prison camps, "re-education centers," and other institutions of terror. Satan creates a close imitation of hell on earth, not simply to increase his power, but because he wishes to imitate God. But he cannot match God. He can kill only the body, not the soul. He wants all men to fear this bodily death above all. This is the opposite of the kingdom of Christ. Jesus said:

> Whatever I tell you in the dark, speak in the light; and what you hear in the ear, preach on the housetops. And do not fear those who kill the body but cannot kill the soul. But rather fear Him who is able to destroy both soul and body in hell (Matthew 10:27-28).

5. Inheritance/Continuity (survival)

Satan wants to build up his kingdom. To do this, he must build his power year after year, generation after generation. But he cannot do this. God always cuts short the kingdoms of evil.

> For I, the LORD your God, am a jealous God, visiting the iniquity of the fathers on the children to the third and fourth generation of those who hate Me, but showing mercy to thousands [of generations — G.N.], to those who love Me and keep My commandments (Exodus 20:5-6).

Thus, Satan must speed up the process. He must take huge risks, the way that gamblers and debtors do. He must do in a few years what the steady preaching of the gospel can accomplish in centuries. Thus, Satan's kingdoms always collapse, whereas Christian culture continues to expand its influence.

Satan can offer his followers no long-term inheritance for their children. God *can* offer His followers a long-term inheritance for their children. God's people can believe in the long-term future; Satan's followers cannot. God's people become *future-oriented*; Satan's people can do so only when heavily influenced by the worldview of Christianity.

Summary

Dominion is by covenant. So is power. Satan's covenant is a poor imitation of God's. He must accomplish through violent revolution, theft, torture, and high risks what God's people can accomplish through steady hard work, thrift, faithfulness, honesty, reliability, and prayer.

The kingdom of God is very different from the kingdom of Marx. Wherever Communists take over, they impose their covenant of power. They imitate God by trying to speed up the processes of history. They work fast, for Satan's time is short (Revelation 12:12). They are doomed in eternity and doomed in history, but they continue to struggle against the limits of God's creation.

That in our day they have been forced to adopt the language of the Bible in order to breathe new hope and new vitality into their program of world conquest testifies to how little time they have left, and how dependent they are on the categories of the Bible. Satan is a thief, a liar, and an imitator. Christians work with the truth. The future belongs to them, not to Marxism.

In summary:

1. Biblical religion is covenantal religion.
2. A Biblical covenant involves a self-maledictory oath.
3. Only three institutions have a God-granted right to impose such oaths: family government, church government, and civil government.
4. The Biblical covenant has five points.
5. Transcendence/immanence says that God is above His creation, yet present with it.
6. Hierarchy/authority says that all human institutions are hierarchical, and we are supposed to place them under God and under His laws.
7. Law/dominion says that we exercise dominion by obeying God's ethical requirements.
8. Judgment/oath says that God is a final judge and continuing judge.
9. Inheritance/continuity says that God will pass the lawful inheritance to the covenantally faithful heirs: heirs of Christ, not Adam.
10. Satan's covenant imitates God's.
11. Satan is neither transcendent (omnipotent) nor immanent (omnipresent).
12. This means that he must compensate for this lack by concentrating power in his hierarchy.
13. He affirms magic or power, not ethics, as tools of dominion.
14. Communists and tyrants imitate God, the final judge, by adopting torture and terror as social policies.
15. God cuts short Satan's earthly kingdoms, transferring their inheritance to His people.
16. Dominion is by covenant.
17. Power is also by covenant.
18. The question is: Whose covenant?

5

THE LIBERATION OF THE INDIVIDUAL

Jesus answered them [the Jews], "Most assuredly, I say to you, whoever commits sin is a slave of sin. And a slave does not abide in the house forever, but a son abides forever. Therefore if the Son makes you free, you shall be free indeed" (John 8:34-36).

Adam was a son of God. He forfeited his sonship when he placed himself ethically under a new ruler, Satan. Christ, the second Adam, came to earth in order to restore this forfeited sonship to His people. It is the Son of God who makes men free. He brings them to God the Father.

Jesus said to him, "I am the way, the truth, and the life. No one comes to the Father except through Me" (John 14:6).

God in His grace adopts people to be part of His *ethical, regenerate* family (John 1:12). They are no longer *disinherited sons*. There is no doubt that there is a universal Fatherhood of God, and a universal brotherhood of man. Men are all brothers—just like Cain and Abel. They are envy-filled, hateful brothers. They are all created as men, in the image of God.

And He has made from one blood every nation of men to dwell on all the earth, and He has determined their preappointed times and the boundaries of their habitation, so that they should seek the Lord, in the hope that they might grope for Him and find Him, though He is not far from each one of us; for in Him we live and move and have our being . . . (Acts 17:26-28a).

The liberal theologians and humanists have drawn deadly conclusions concerning the universal Fatherhood of God and the universal brotherhood of man. Such a brotherhood is a *brotherhood of condemnation*. It is mandatory ethically that each person escape from this brotherhood. It is adopted sonship, not created sonship, that alone offers eternal life and eternal hope.

Liberation Inward

Christians preach the gospel to the lost. We assume that there is a *point of contact* between the saved and the lost. If there weren't, how could saved and lost communicate? There is such a point of contact: the image of God in all men. But the unbeliever suppresses this truth.

> For the wrath of God is revealed from heaven against all ungodliness and unrighteousness of men, who suppress [hold back] the truth in unrighteousness (Romans 1:18).

This is *active ignorance*. Unregenerate people suppress the testimony of the creation, including the testimony of their own being, to God and God's wrath.

> For the message of the cross is foolishness to those who are perishing, but to us who are being saved it is the power of God (1 Corinthians 1:18).

> But the natural man does not receive the things of the Spirit of God, for they are foolishness to him; nor can he know them, because they are spiritually discerned. But he that is spiritual judges all things, yet he himself is judged by no one. For "Who has known the mind of the Lord that he may instruct Him?" But we have the mind of Christ (1 Corinthians 2:14-16).

Then how can the unregenerate man receive the things of the Spirit? How can he be set free? By the grace of God. This is the only way he can be set free. He must be *given* the mind of Christ. The righteousness of Christ is imputed to him, not for any work that he does, but simply by God's grace.

> For by grace you have been saved through faith, and that not of yourselves; it is the gift of God, not of works, lest anyone should boast (Ephesians 2:8-9).

Liberation Outward

But we are not saved to sit idly, waiting for Jesus to come from heaven and deliver us from all problems. We have been saved, Paul goes on to say, in order to walk in the good works that God has prepared beforehand for us:

> For we are His workmanship, created in Christ Jesus for good works, which God prepared beforehand that we should walk in them (Ephesians 2:10).

An important goal of personal liberation is outward liberation. Redeemed men are to begin to transform the world around them by their good works. They are to bear good fruit. Jesus warned:

> Beware of false prophets, who come to you in sheep's clothing, but inwardly they are ravenous wolves. You will know them by their fruits. Do men gather grapes from thornbushes or figs from thistles? Even so, every good tree bears good fruit, but a bad tree bears bad fruit. A good tree cannot bear bad fruit, nor can a bad tree bear good fruit. Every tree that does not bear good fruit is cut down and thrown into the fire. Therefore by their fruits you shall know them (Matthew 7:15-20).

False Liberation

The Marxist liberation theologians come before men, claiming to be Christians. They claim they are preaching God's program of violent revolution, re-education, top-down state planning, military expansion, and the abolition of private property.

Wherever Marxism is imposed, the standard of living falls, refugees flee across borders in abject poverty, and the barbed wire and walls go up along the borders. The leaders of the revolution need to force people to stay inside the borders of paradise. Why? Because Marxism is a classic case of poison fruit. Marxist liberation theologians are the classic case, perhaps in the history of man, of wolves in sheep's clothing. The fruit is bad because Marxism is evil. There is no other word for it: *evil*. It destroys men and societies in the name of liberation. It offers false hopes, and then smashes those who listen. In the case of every known Marxist revolution, the surviving leaders imprison or execute their former "comrades." *The revolution eats its own children.* (But not soon enough!) This has been a theme in human literature from the beginning. In Greek mythology, Chronos is the god who ate his children. One child escaped (Zeus), and later destroyed Chronos. Chronos was the god of time, known in Roman mythology as Saturn, the god of revolution. He was the god of the chaos festival: saturnalia. (We still call the seventh day of the week Saturday.)

What is the heart of the error of all false religions? That man's own works can save him. This is the dead end for mankind. Men are already under judgment in Adam. They need grace, not works, to deliver them back into the household of God.

Environmental Determinism

A related error is *environmental determinism*. Men blame their environment for their sin. When God came to Adam and asked him if he had eaten the forbidden fruit, what did Adam say? "The woman whom You gave to me, she gave me of the tree, and I did eat" (Genesis 3:12). Then God confronted the woman. What did she say? "The serpent deceived me, and I ate" (v. 13). In short, "You did it, God. It's really your fault. You gave us a poor environment. You kept saying that it was good, but it wasn't good. It allowed us to sin." They blamed God for their sin.

Satan, of course, said nothing, for God asked him nothing. Satan was cursed. Adam and Eve were punished. The ground was cursed. God is not an environmental determinist. He blames sinners for their sin (Romans 9:14-23).

Marxism is perhaps the most successful religion of environmental determinism in man's history. The Marxist believes that positive change in society can come only when key impersonal forces of history are present. The good intentions of men are worth nothing. Only historical forces count. Marx was quite clear about this in his famous Preface to his 1859 book (the year that Darwin's *Origin of Species* appeared), *A Contribution to the Critique of Political Economy.* (This is a lengthy and highly theoretical passage, but the whole world has been turned upside down by it.)

The general result at which I arrived and which, once won, served as a guiding thread for my studies, can be briefly formulated as follows: In the social production of their life, men enter into definite relations that are indispensable and independent of their will, relations of production which correspond to a definite stage of development of their material productive forces. The sum total of these relations of production constitutes the economic structure of society, the real foundation, on which rises a legal and political superstructure and to which correspond definite forms of social consciousness. The mode of production of material life conditions the social, political and intellectual life process in general. It is not the consciousness of men that determines their being, but, on the contrary, their social being that determines their consciousness. At a certain stage of their development, the material productive forces of society come in conflict with the existing relations of production, or—what is but a legal expression for the same thing—with the property relations within which they have been at work hitherto. From forms of development of the productive forces these relations turn into their fetters. Then begins an epoch of social revolution. . . . No social order ever perishes before all the productive forces for which there is room in it have developed; and new, higher relations of production never appear before the material conditions of their existence have matured in the womb of the old society itself. Therefore mankind always sets itself only such tasks as it can solve; since, looking at the matter more closely, it will always be found that the task itself arises only when the material conditions for its solution already exist or are at least in the process of formation.

The material forces of production create a society's religious, intellectual, and cultural "superstructure." Then changes in the economic "substructure" come into conflict with the existing superstructure. This produces a social revolution: slavery to feudalism, feudalism to capitalism, capitalism to socialism, socialism to communism.

Unfortunately for this theory, Communist revolutions almost always take place in rural feudal societies, not in capitalist societies where Marx's theory says that they must. The revolution never happens in capitalist societies except shortly after a lost war, and then these revolutions are overturned. But I am not here to discuss the failures of Marxist theory, which are legion. I have done that job elsewhere.[1] This book is about liberation theology.

Marxist liberation theology teaches that man's nature is changed *as a result of the revolution*. The change in man's nature is *outside-in*. This is the essence of Satanism. This is pure environmental determinism, right out of the mouth of Adam after his rebellion. The Satanists want to create a new humanity through social engineering and the transformation of the social, political, and economic environment. The creation of a new humanity is a religious impulse, mimicking the Bible. The Bible preaches *ethical reconciliation* — a new humanity born by God's imputation of Christ's perfect humanity (though *not* His divinity) to individual sinners. This is to lead to evangelism: inside-out ethical renovation that produces the spread of reconciliation.

> Therefore, if anyone is in Christ, he is a new creation; old things have passed away; behold, all things have become new. Now all things are of God, who has reconciled us to Himself through Jesus Christ, and has given us the ministry of reconciliation, that is, that God was in Christ reconciling the world to Himself, not imputing their trespasses to them, and has committed to us the word of reconciliation. Therefore we are ambassadors for Christ, as though God were pleading through us: we implore you on Christ's behalf, be reconciled to God (2 Corinthians 5:17-20).

Outside-in

Compare Paul's vision of personal regeneration, voluntarism, evangelism, and world service as ambassadors of a risen Christ with the *outside-in* remaking of mankind that is recommended by Marxist liberation theologian José Miranda:

> Our revolution is directed toward the creation of the new human being. But unlike the attackers, we seek to posit the necessary means for the formation of this new human being. And the in-

---

1. Gary North, *Marx's Religion of Revolution: The Doctrine of Creative Destruction* (Nutley, New Jersey: Craig Press, 1968).

dispensible means is a new social structure. Is it not perfectly obvious that an existing social system has more efficacy for education or miseducation than the exhortations of classroom or temple? How far can you get with the idea that a person should not place his or her heart in money and material things (the central idea of the Sermon on the Mount) if the existing social system inculcates just the contrary under pain of blows and death? Perhaps an insignificant minority can heroically resist the peremptory mandates of such a system. But Christianity cares about all human beings. It cannot content itself with saving a tiny minority. The majority cannot even assign a sense of realism to the Christian message of brotherhood and solidarity with neighbor, when the social structure imposes on it, under pain of annihilation, the task of seeking its proper interest and letting the chips fall where they may, without preoccupying itself with other people. Structural change will be a mere means for personal change—but a means so obviously necessary, that those who fail to give it first priority demonstrate by that very fact that their vaunted desire to transform persons is just empty rhetoric.[2]

Not to put too fine a point to it, but how does this prophet for Communism think that the message and work of Jesus and the disciples led to the transformation of the Roman Empire? What means of comprehensive "structural alterations" of Mediterranean society did that tiny band of disciples possess? All they had was the truth, the empowering of the Holy Spirit, and a long-term vision of the kingdom of God.

What small groups of dedicated Christians need today, Miranda might say in a moment of candor, is a cadre of trained revolutionaries supported with weapons from the Soviet Union, by way of Cuba. As it is, he devoted Chapter 3 of his three-chapter book to the topic, "Politics and Violence in Jesus of Nazareth."

This view of man leads to the creation of a massive central planning system, run by an elite, and imposed by force in a top-

---

2. Miranda, *Communism in the Bible* (Maryknoll, New York: Orbis, [1981] 1982), p. 6.

down fashion. This is the pyramid of power. "Man must remake man!" This means that *a few men* must remake all the others.

Self-Government Under God

When we say "government," we usually have in mind the state, meaning civil government. But civil government is not by any means the only form of government. There is family government and church government, too. But most important of all is *self*-government.

In bringing up children, especially in a large family, how could parents manage if the children did not mature as they grow older? If each child took as much careful attention and close observation as a three-year-old, it would be nearly impossible to do a good job. The hope of every parent is that as each child grows older, he will become more wise, meaning self-disciplined.

This is true of every organization except insane asylums. Whether we are speaking about an army, a police force, a family, a school, or a business, if those people with long experience fail to exercise self-government, the organization breaks down. What this means is that those at the top cannot spend the resources necessary for monitoring the behavior and performance of all those under them. No organization has that many spare resources. Those at the top issue general rules — make good grades in school, make a profit in business, grow a crop, clean up your room, etc. — and then monitor people's performance once in a while. The emphasis is on increasing the extent of individual decision-making, in contrast to bureaucracy's system of reducing the zones of freedom. God's hierarchy is a *bottom-up* system, an appeals court.

Because God is all-seeing, He can monitor our performance continually. Yet even God restrains Himself. He brings judgment from time to time in every person's life, but He does not stand at our sides yelling orders in our ears. He expects us to become mature in the faith. This means that we must increase our own self-monitoring under God's law-order and in terms of our specific goals for our lives.

This means that government is to serve as a sort of appeals court. It begins in the family. "Dad, he took my ball!" "She hit me!" "He said he would help me clean the kitchen if I helped him with his homework!" And so on. Parents serve as referees. So do policemen, judges, and pastors. The basic model is in Exodus 18, where Jethro, Moses' father-in-law, told him to appoint righteous men as judges over the people, so that only the hard cases would come up the chain of command.

Satan's hierarchy is different. It, too, is a chain of command. It, too, resembles a pyramid. But it is a *top-down* command structure, a bureaucracy rather than an appeals court system. If he had his way, Satan would monitor everything we do. Unlike God, he trusts no one, since he himself is untrustworthy. So we see in all satanic administrations an attempt to substitute massive bureaucracy for self-government.

Satan has no permanent law-order. He keeps changing the rules. (In this sense, the Marxist explanation of historical change is totally satanic: all laws are said to change according to the historical era and the mode of production.) Thus, Satan must monitor everyone under him, for there are no fixed standards by which his subordinates can judge their performance or their rewards or punishments from superiors.

Hierarchy in Satan's kingdoms is everything, for he is neither all-powerful nor all-seeing. Self-government counts for very little. The less of it, the better, in Satan's view. And yet he needs it, for he is not God. He cannot monitor everything and everyone, as God can. So he is forced to rely on an aspect of God's creation and God's covenanted order if he wishes to achieve his evil goals. He cannot be fully consistent with his own desires and standards if he wishes to exercise power. He has to steal huge chunks of God's system even to function. He is a creature; he remains dependent on God.

Thus, when the Christian thinks "government," he should instantly think, "self-government under God's law." This is true liberation theology, and the basis of God-blessed, long-term dominion.

Summary

What we have here is a conflict in worldviews. The dominion religion of the Bible cannot be reconciled with the power religion of the Marxists. They both aim at regeneration, both personal and institutional. They both hold out a vision of a better life on earth. They both offer men hope that their efforts will count for something, not just on the day of judgment, but in history. The escape religion has little to offer either the dominionists or the power-seekers.

The differences between the two systems are many. Who is sovereign in the process of ethical transformation, God or man? Who changes men's hearts, God or man? What is the means of personal transformation, the preaching of the gospel of *personal, individual* salvation, or the imposition by force of an elitist, top-down revolutionary cadre? Is the revolution an inside-out process, or an outside-in process?

Both groups want to alter existing social institutions. Dominion religion preaches steady transformation by means of dominion; power religion preaches a need for rapid change, including revolution. Satan knows that his time is short. He also knows that God cuts off the growth of his kingdoms every few generations, transferring their wealth to Christians. Israel inherits Canaan.

The problem comes when, incredibly, the two groups switch their time perspective. Christians in this century have waited for Jesus to return and overnight set up His total kingdom. Communists, on the other hand, work long and hard, generation after generation, to establish the conditions favorable for Communist revolution. The Christians have become short-run in perspective, while the Communists have become long-run. Thus, the Communists have made far more of a mark on the twentieth century, and have spread their control very rapidly. Christians, thinking short run and thinking other worldly, have been on the defensive.

If, as now seems possible, increasing numbers of Christians return in the next few years to their original heritage of future-orientation, hard work, long-term planning, and self-discipline, we will see a reversal of the spread of Marxism and other forms of man-exalting humanism. But the change must come in people's minds before it comes to their institutional arrangements. Christianity preaches an inside-out theory of social change. The only way to sustain God's cultural blessings is through the spread of the soul-saving gospel of Christ, person by person.

In summary:

1. Human freedom comes from regeneration by God.
2. This means adoption out of Adam's fallen family into Christ's ethical family.
3. The Fatherhood of God and the brotherhood of man point to final judgment: disinherited sons of Adam.
4. Liberation begins inside man: regeneration.
5. Those who do not believe in Christ are people who actively suppress the testimony of nature to the coming wrath of God.
6. Men must be regenerated before they can respond in faith to the gospel.
7. When converted, men begin to alter their lives to conform increasingly to God's law.
8. Liberation spreads outward from men's hearts to men's institutions.
9. Marxism preaches environmental determinism.
10. Marxists teach that men's social environments must change before mankind can change.
11. Their goal is the creation of a new humanity.
12. This is to be accomplished by revolution, tyranny, social engineering, and re-education (indoctrination).
13. The state is the agency of central planning and coercion.
14. The Biblical concept of government rests on the existence of self-government under God.
15. Maturing in the Christian faith means greater amounts of self-government.
16. This means increasing the zones of individual decision-making.
17. Biblical hierarchies are essentially appeals courts.
18. In Satan's kingdoms, hierarchies are top-down bureaucracies.
19. These rival worldviews cannot successfully be reconciled.

6

THE LIBERATION OF THE FAMILY

> Honor your father and your mother: that your days may be long
> on the land which the LORD your God is giving you (Exodus 20:12).

The family is a covenantal institution. Marriage vows under God involve taking self-maledictory oaths: husband and wife swear loyalty to each other, with the death penalty for adultery hanging over them (Leviticus 20:10). They say in Christian ceremonies, "till death do us part."

The family covenant is structured along the same lines as God's covenant structure. It begins with transcendence and immanence (presence). God's transcendence and presence are seen in the representative position of the father as God's lawful family agent.

> Wives, submit to your own husbands as to the Lord. For the
> husband is head of the wife, as also Christ is head of the church;
> and He is the Savior of the body. Therefore, just as the church is
> subject to Christ, so let the wives be to their own husbands in
> everything (Ephesians 5:22-24).

There is a hierarchy in the family: husbands over wives; parents over children (Ephesians 6:1-3).

There is law in the family: the parents under God teach the children daily in God's law (Deuteronomy 6:6-7).

There is judgment in the family: parents are required to inflict punishments, even physical pain, in order to train children in godliness.

Finally, there is inheritance. The children, if they are obedient

73

to the parents and reliable stewards, are supposed to benefit from the efforts of the parents. Family capital is to increase down through the generations of the godly.

In short, there is a family version of the general covenant structure outlined in Chapter 4.

Similarly, there is a satanic imitation. The state, as the highest form of visible human power, has begun to replace the family in all of these five areas. The state in Marxist nations gets children to inform on parents, making them the representatives of the new god.

The state imposes a hierarchy over families. The father answers to the state.

The state establishes its law and teaches the children in compulsory schools.

The state takes the right to punish children from parents and transfers it to specialized agents of the state.

Finally, the state taxes away the inheritance of families. It decapitalizes Christian families, thereby making it far more difficult for Christians to build up a growing capital base for dominion over the generations.

We see the ancient war between Christ and Satan in the modern war over who owns the family. (See Ray Sutton's book in the Biblical Blueprints Series, *Who Owns the Family? God or the State?*)

Long Life

Paul tells us that the fifth commandment is the first commandment to which a promise is attached (Ephesians 6:3). What does it mean, "that your days may be long in the land which the LORD your God is giving you"? It is a promise given to the *nation*. It is a collective promise, not an individual promise as such.

God does not promise that every single child who shows honor for his parents will enjoy long life, nor does He assure us that every single dishonoring child will die young. Esau went against his parents' wishes when he married a Canaanite women (Genesis 26:34-35), yet he lived to be at least 120, for he and Jacob buried Isaac, who had died at age 180 (Genesis 35:29), and they had been born when Isaac was 60 years old (Genesis 25:26). Joseph was alive at this time, and the Bible speaks of Joseph as the son of Jacob's old age (Genesis 37:3). In the case of Esau, a dishonoring child lived into old age. Abel, who honored God, and who presumably honored his parents as God's representatives, was slain by his violent brother, who in turn survived to establish a pagan civilization (Genesis 4).

What God does promise is that a *society* in which the *majority* of men do honor their parents will be marked by the long life expectancy of its members. This longer lifespan will be statistically significant. The society will enjoy, for example, lower life insurance premiums in every age bracket compared with the premiums in cultures that are marked by rebellion against parents. In other words, the risk of death in any given year will be lower, statistically, for the average member of that age bracket. Some will die, of course, but not as many as those who die at the same age in a parent-dishonoring culture.

Long Life and Dominion

The promise is significant. It offers long life. The very first promise that is connected to a commandment is long life. This indicates men's desire to survive into old age. *Men want to live.* It is a universal desire, though it is marred or distorted by the effects of sin. All those who hate God love death (Proverbs 8:36). Nevertheless, a standard expression of honor in the ancient Near East, especially in pagan civilizations, was reserved for the king: "O king, live forever" (Daniel 2:4; 5:10; 6:21). When God attached this particular blessing to this commandment, He could be assured of its initial attractiveness in the eyes of men. Life is a blessing for the faithful, and it is desired even by the unfaithful. It is not a burden to be borne patiently by steadfast "pilgrims" who are stoically "passing through life." Life is not just something to pass the time away. It is a *positive blessing.*

We know that the promise to Abraham was that he would have many children, meaning heirs throughout time (Genesis 17:4-6). We know that a large family is a blessing (Psalm 127:3-5).

We know that one of the promised blessings for the godly is that miscarriages will be reduced in a nation which is seeking to conform itself to God's law (Exodus 23:26). The demographic implication of the Biblical perspective should be obvious: *a large and growing population.* When godliness simultaneously increases both the birth rate and the survival rate, the godly society will experience a population explosion. What God sets forth in His word is simple enough, though both Christians and pagans in the late twentieth century have refused to believe it: *one sign of His pleasure with His people is a population explosion.*

Population growth is not a *guarantee* of His pleasure. Ungodly societies can temporarily sustain a population explosion, especially when they have become the recipients of the blessings of God's law (for example, Western medical technology) apart from the ethical foundations that sustain these blessings. Nevertheless, sustained population growth over many generations is one of God's external blessings, and these blessings cannot be sustained long-term apart from conformity to at least the external, civil, and institutional requirements of God's law.

Long life is a biological foretaste of eternal life. It is an earthly "down payment" (earnest) by God. It points to eternal life. It is also a capital asset which enables men to labor longer in their assigned task of subduing their portion of the earth to God's glory. *Long life is an integral part of the dominion covenant.*

Since the fulfillment of the dominion covenant involves filling the earth, it is understandable why long life should be so important. It is one critical factor in the population expansion necessary to fulfill the terms of that covenant, the other being high birth rates. God has pointed clearly to the importance of the family in fulfilling the terms of the dominion covenant. The parents receive the blessing of children (high birth rate), and the children secure long life by honoring their parents. Or, to put it even more plainly, a man gains the blessing of long life, including the ability to produce a large family, by honoring his parents. The way in which the people of a culture define and practice their family obligations will determine their ability to approach the earthly fulfillment of the dominion covenant. Without a close adherence to this, the fifth commandment, no society can hope to receive and *keep* the capital necessary to fulfill the terms of the dominion covenant, especially the human capital involved in a population explosion.

Parental Sovereignty

Parents possess limited, but completely legitimate, derivative sovereignty over their children during the formative years of the children's lives. When children reach the age of civil responsibility, one sign of their maturity is their willingness to establish families of their own (Genesis 2:24). Responsibility therefore steadily shifts as time goes on. Eventually, the aged parents transfer economic and other responsibility to their children, who care for them when they are no longer able to care for themselves. The man in his peak production years may have two-way financial responsibilities: to his parents and to his children. Maximum responsibility hits at an age when, because of economic and biological patterns, a man attains his maximum strength. This shift of responsibility is mandatory, given the mortality of mankind. The Bible provides guidelines for the proper transfer of family responsibility over time.

The requirement that men honor their parents preserves the *continuity of the covenantal family,* and therefore it preserves the *continuity of responsibility.* The totally atomistic family unit is probably impossible; where it exists, the culture which has created it will collapse. *Mutual obligations* bind the family units together. Parents have an obligation to lay up wealth for their children: ". . . for the children ought not to lay up for the parents, but the parents for the children" (2 Corinthians 12:14b). Parents are not to squander their children's inheritance.

The Double Portion

It should also be recognized that each of the children has a legitimate claim to part of the patrimony, unless disinherited because of his rebellion against parents or his personal immorality. The eldest son is entitled to a double portion of the estate (Deuteronomy 21:15-17). Why does the eldest son inherit this double portion? A reasonable explanation is that he is the person with the primary responsibility for the care of his parents.

The English system of primogeniture, in which the eldest son inherited all of the landed estate, was clearly unbiblical, and the breakdown of that system in the nineteenth century was a step forward. Such a system places too much responsibility on the eldest son, leaving the other children bereft of capital, but also psychologically free of economic obligations toward the parents. It cuts off most of the children from the mutual obligations of the covenantal family.

Economic obligations should flow in both directions: toward the children in the early years, toward the parents in the later years, and back toward the children at the death of the parents, when the family's capital is inherited by the survivors. In short, children inherit, but parents must first be provided for.

The Continuity of Capital

The Biblical law-order is a unity. Blessings and responsibilities are linked. Without the coherence of comprehensive Biblical law, blessings can become *curses*. We have a good example of this in this commandment. Assume that a son honors his parents during their lifetime. He receives the blessing of long life. At the same time, he is not careful to teach his own children the requirements of this commandment. He wastes his own estate, neglecting the spiritual education of his children. He has nothing to live on in his old age. His fortune is gone, and his own children know it. The break in the family between generations is now a threat to him. Knowing that he has abandoned them by squandering the family estate, his children abandon him to poverty in his old age, when he most needs assistance. The blessing of long life then becomes a curse to him. He slowly rots away in abject poverty.

Capital, if familistic in nature, is less likely to be squandered. In a truly godly social order, the familiar rags-to-riches-to-rags progression of three generations, from grandfather to grandchildren, is not supposed to become typical, despite the fact that the *legal possibility* of "rags-to-riches-to-rags" is basic to the preservation of a free society. The example of a man who pulls himself up out of poverty, only to see his children squander his fortune, leaving his grandchildren destitute, is neither normative nor normal in a Christian social order. The godly do not lay up treasure for the ungodly; the reverse is true (Proverbs 13:22). *Wealth in the long run flows toward provident and productive citizens who exercise dominion in terms of Biblical law.* Therefore, these dual obligations, from fathers to sons and from sons to fathers, are an important aspect of the Biblical tendency toward economic growth over many generations.

Fathers have economic incentives to expand the family's capital base, and they also have an incentive to train up children who will not dissipate the family's capital. The *continuity of capital*, under God's law, is promoted by the laws of inheritance-honor. This preservation of capital is crucial for long-term economic development.

In order to preserve family capital over time, godly parents must train their children to follow the ethical standards of the Bible. The Biblical basis for long-term expansion of family capital is ethical: *character* and *competence*. But this ethical foundation for long-term family capital growth is not acceptable to anti-Biblical cultures. They want the fruits of Christian culture without the roots. Thus, we find that civil governments often take steps to preserve *already existing* family fortunes at the expense of those productive families that are ready and willing to make their economic contribution to the production process. A phenomenon that is supposed to be the product of ethics and education—the expansion of family capital over many generations—is *temporarily* produced by the use of State power. This substitution of power for ethics is characteristic of Satan's religions—not power as the product of Biblical ethics ("right eventually produces might"), but power as an alternative to Biblical ethics ("might makes right").

Compound Economic Growth

The importance of the continuity of capital can be seen in any example involving compound interest. Let me say from the beginning, we cannot expect to see this compound interest phenomenon continue uninterrupted in any family forever. We also cannot expect to see rates of growth over 1% for centuries at a time. As I like to point out, the 4 billion people on earth in 1980 would multiply to over 83 trillion in a thousand years, if the rate of population growth were 1% per annum. But the fact remains, the longer the compound growth phenomenon continues, the smaller the annual percentage increase needs to be in order to produce spectacular results.

Let us assume that we are dealing with a given monetary unit. We can call it a *talent*. A young married man begins with 100 talents. Say that he multiplies this capital base by 2% per annum. At the end of 50 years, the couple has 269 talents. Let us assume that the family, and their children's families, multiply at 1% per annum, on the average, throughout each subsequent family's lifetime. After 250 years, if the growth rates both of people and capital persist, the total family capital base is up to 14,126 talents. Divided by 24 heirs, each husband or wife now has 589 talents. This is almost a 6-fold increase per family unit, which is considerable. We now have 24 family units, even assuming that each heir has married someone who has brought no capital into the marriage, with almost six times the wealth that the original family started out with.

What if the capital base should increase by 3%? At the end of 50 years, the original couple would have 438 talents, over a 4-fold increase. This is quite impressive. But at the end of 250 years, the family would possess 161,922 talents, over 1,600 times as large. Even divided by 24 family units, the per family capital base would be 6,747 talents, or almost 68 times as great.

Consider the implications of these figures. A future-oriented man—a man like Abraham—could look forward to his heirs' possessing vastly greater wealth than he ever could hope to attain personally. Yet this is the kind of vision God offers His people, just as He offered it to Abraham: heirs two or three generations later who will be numerous and rich. God offers a man the hope of substantially increased wealth during his own lifetime, in response to his covenantal faithfulness, hard work, and thrift.

God also offers the covenantal society truly vast increases in per family wealth, if the terms of the covenant are maintained. The covenant community increases its control of capital, generation by generation, piling up ever-greater quantities of capital, until the growth becomes exponential, meaning astronomical, meaning impossible. Compound growth therefore points to the fulfillment of the dominion covenant, the subduing of the earth. It points to the end of cursed time.

(It might be appropriate at this point to clarify what I mean when I speak about a covenant society amassing huge numbers of monetary units called talents. If we are speaking of a whole society, and not just a single family, then for all of them to amass 6,747 talents per family in 250 years, there would have to be mass inflation, the printing of billions of "talent notes." I am speaking not of physical slips of paper called talents; I am speaking of goods and services of *value*. The 100 talents per family, multiplied by all the families in the society, would not be allowed to increase; *prices would fall* in response to increased production of 3% per annum. Eventually, if the whole society experiences 3% per annum economic growth, given a fixed money supply, prices would begin to approach zero. But prices in a cursed world will never reach zero; there will always be economic scarcity [Genesis 3:17-19]. In fact, scarcity is defined as a universe in which total demand is greater than supply at zero price. So the assumption of permanent compound economic growth is incorrect. Either the growth process stops in the aggregate, or else time ends. That, of course, is precisely the point. Time *will* end.)

A man whose vision is geared to dominion, in time and on earth, has to look to the years beyond his lifetime. He cannot hope to build up his family's capital base in his own lifetime sufficient to achieve conquest. (Yes, a few men do achieve this, but not many; we are talking about dominion by the Christian community, not the dominion of a few families.) If he looks two or more centuries into the future, it becomes a conceivable task.

If a man's time perspective is limited to his own lifetime, then he must either give up the idea of family dominion, or else he must adopt the mentality of the gambler. He has to "go for the big pay-off." He must sacrifice everything for capital expansion, risking everything he has, plus vast quantities of borrowed money, on untried, high-risk, high-return ventures. He must abandon everything conventional, for an investor earns only conventional returns (prevailing interest rate) from conventional ventures. The man's world becomes an endless series of all-or-nothing decisions.

Trusteeship: Which Family?

The continuity of capital is obviously threatened by the rise of the familistic state. It establishes itself as the trustee for all men, from womb to tomb. It is therefore entitled to support by those who receive its protection. Like a father, or better yet, like a distant uncle who guides the fortunes of an orphaned nephew, the state must administer the funds, always taking a large portion of those funds as a necessary fee for service performed.

As men steadily begin to perceive the implications of the familistic state, they seek to hide their assets from its tax collectors. Men try to find ways to pass along wealth to their heirs, and the state relentlessly searches for ways of closing off escape hatches. The new "parent" must not be deprived of its support from every member of the family. And once the capital is collected, it is dissipated in a wave of corruption, mismanagement, bureaucratic salaries, and politically motivated compulsory charity programs. Men see the erosion of their capital, and they seek to hide it away. They recognize what the pseudo-family of the state will do to the inheritance of their children. Still, because of entrenched envy, they do not turn back. They and their parents and grandparents accepted the philosophical justifications of "soaking the rich" by means of the ballot box, but now that price inflation has pushed everyone into higher tax brackets, they are horrified by what they find. They have now been snared themselves, but they seem unable to turn back, for to turn back would involve an admission of the immorality and inefficiency of the "soak the rich" programs of twentieth-century democratic politics.

The modern messianic state would like to make permanent

children of its wards. This is a primary justification for the state's existence today. It must administer the inheritance for the benefit of children. But the children are *perpetual servants*, increasingly dependent upon the coercive wealth redistribution of politics. They become a growing army of dependents. The state's bureaucrats do not recognize what every human parent must eventually recognize, namely, that he is going to become weak, and that he must encourage independence on the part of his heirs if he is to secure safety for himself in his old age. The state, by making men permanent children, guarantees its own demise, for the children cannot forever support the "trustee state," if the state has, in effect, institutionalized the voters.

The family *is* a trustee. By acknowledging the legitimacy of the laws of the family, men honor God, although the unregenerate do so unwittingly and in spite of their professed theology of autonomy before God. External blessings flow to those who honor God's laws. By establishing a tradition of honoring parents, sons increase the likelihood that in their old age their own children will protect them from the burdens of old age. The risks that life poses to the old are therefore minimized. The familistic welfare structure is *reciprocal* and *personal*. It is undergirded by revealed law and by family tradition. It need not rely heavily on the far weaker support of sentiment—an important aspect of the religion of humanism. The growth of capital within the family increases each succeeding generation's ability to conquer nature to the glory of God, including the infirmities and vulnerabilities of old age.

The State as Kidnapper

The statist pseudo-family cannot permit this sort of challenge to its self-proclaimed sovereignty. The modern state has therefore laid claim to ownership of the children through the tax-supported public school system. Children are obviously a form of family capital. They are to be trained, which involves costs to the parents. But the parents have a legitimate claim on a portion of the future assets of the children. The relationship involves costs and benefits for both generations. Neither side needs to buy the love of the other, any more than men need to buy the love of God. Each generation gives, and each receives. The relationship is both personal and economic.

But today the modern state intervenes. It provides the children's education. It lays claim to future payments (taxes) by the children when they have reached maturity. Of necessity, it must try to buy the love (votes) of those children when they reach maturity. The children often remain subservient to the state-parent, unwilling to launch independent lives of their own, given the costs of breaking the financial and emotional tie with the welfare office. The covenant family's resource, the children, are stolen by the modern state. The state promises old age support. The state promises health care for the aged. The state provides state-financed and state-licensed education for the young. The state attempts to replace the benefits of the family, and simultaneously must require the same sort of financial support from the adults during their productive years. The relationship is impersonal and economic. The relationship is, by law, bureaucratic.

Destroying Inheritance

This disastrous attempt of the civil government to replace the functions of the covenant family eventually destroys the productive mutual relationships between generations. It destroys the personal bond, making the *young in general* legally responsible for the *old in general*. The family name—so central to the life of a godly social order—is erased, and computerized numbers are substituted. The incentives for families to preserve their capital, whether for old age or for generations into the future, are reduced, for each generation's economic future is no longer legally bound to the success and prosperity of the children. "Eat, drink, and be merry, for tomorrow there will be government checks." But the dissipation of family capital, when it becomes a culture-wide phenomenon, destroys economic productivity, which in turn destroys the tax base of the state. The state cannot write the promised checks, or if it does, the monetary unit steadily grows worthless, as fiat money inflates the price level.

By abandoning the principle of family responsibility, the modern messianic state wastes a culture's capital, destroys inheritance, and makes more acceptable both euthanasia (which reduces the expense of caring for the unproductive elderly) and abortion (which reduces the expense of training and caring for the unproductive young). Lawless men, in their productive years, refuse to share their wealth with dying parents and squalling children. They look only at present costs, neglecting future benefits, such as the care which the unborn might provide them in their old age. *They have faith in the compassionate and productive state*, the great social myth of the twentieth century. They want its benefits, but they never ask themselves the key question: *Who will pay* for their retirement years? The shrinking number of children, who are even more present-oriented, even more conditioned by the statist educational system, even more unwilling to share their wealth with the now-unproductive aged of the land? With the dissipation of capital, the productive voters will resist the demands of the elderly. *The generations go to war against one another: the war of politics.*

The Coming Bankruptcy

The pseudo-family state is an agent of social, political, and economic bankruptcy. It still has its intellectual defenders, even within the Christian community, although its defenders tend to be products of the state-supported, state-certified, and state-aggrandizing universities. *This pseudo-family is suicidal.* It destroys the foundations of productivity, and productivity is the source of all voluntary charity. It is a suicidal family which will pay off its debts with inflated fiat currency. Its compassion will be limited to paper and ink.

The impersonalism of the modern pseudo-family, along with its present-orientation — a vision no longer than the next election — will produce massive, universal failure. It has already done so. The great economic experiment of the twentieth century is almost over, and all the college-level textbooks in economics, political science, and sociology will not be able to justify the system once it erodes the productivity which every parasitic structure requires for its own survival. Like the Canaanitic cultures of Joshua's day, the end is in sight for the modern, messianic, welfare state economies. They have decapitalized their envy-driven, guilt-ridden citizens.

Summary

We see in the family a war between Satan and God, between the rival forms of the covenant. It is imperative for Christians to abandon the religion of humanism. It is imperative that they fulfill their responsibilities as members of a covenantal community. It is imperative that they see to it that their old people, as well as their young people, are not in any way dependent upon the services of a declining welfare state. To become dependent on such an institution is to become a slave. Worse than that: it is to become dependent on a master whose resources are almost spent. When men and women honor their fathers and mothers — financially, spiritually, and institutionally — they will have begun the painful but mandatory journey out of slavery. They will have begun to amass family capital for yet unborn generations.

We must decapitalize the state. The alternative is for the state to decapitalize us. If we are dependent on the state for its support, we are necessarily fostering the decapitalization of the family. *The first and crucial step in decapitalizing the state is to cease calling for favors from the state.* It is to create alternative, voluntary, Biblical institutions that will replace the pseudo-compassion of the messianic state. If the covenant communities refuse to accept this challenge, then they will see their capital dissipated by the spendthrift managers of the humanistic state.

In summary:

1. The covenantal promises of God are collective, not always personal.

2. Honoring parents produces longer lifespans for most people in a society.

3. Longer lifespans can produce a growing population.

4. A growing population is a tool of dominion: "Be fruitful and multiply."

5. Parents possess a God-given, limited, but institutionally

primary responsibility over their children.

6. Over the years, because of aging, responsibility shifts from parents to children.

7. Responsibility is therefore reciprocal over time.

8. Parents and children have mutual responsibilities over time.

9. The eldest son receives a double portion: of the inheritance and of responsibility for caring for aged parents.

10. The Bible teaches the continuity of capital over generations.

11. Family capital is less likely to be wasted.

12. Wealth flows toward provident and productive people in a free society.

13. Parents must train children in competence and character if family capital is to be increased over generations.

14. Compound economic growth produces huge increases in wealth and productivity if even small increases go on for centuries.

15. Christians should view capital as a trust from God, to be handed down and multiplied over time.

16. There are two rival families today: the state and the Christian family unit.

17. The state is increasingly increasing its power and influence (through tax spending) over matters once directed by families and especially fathers.

18. Citizens are seen by state bureaucrats as perpetual slaves and perpetual children.

19. The state has become a kidnapper.

20. The state is destroying the inheritance of families through taxation and controls.

21. The state is squandering the nation's capital.

22. Social, political, and economic bankruptcies are coming when the state can no longer pretend to be God.

23. Christians must abandon the religion of humanism.

24. They must abandon their belief in the state as the true family.

7

THE LIBERATION OF THE CHURCH

> But when he [Uzziah, king of Judah] was strong his heart was
> lifted up, to his destruction, for he transgressed against the LORD
> his God by entering the temple of the LORD to burn incense
> (2 Chronicles 26:16).

The story of Uzziah is not well known. He was a good king
generally (2 Chronicles 26:4) — one of the few good kings in ancient
Israel. But he grew arrogant, as Saul did when he offered a sacrifice to God when Samuel delayed, and lost his kingdom as a result
(1 Samuel 13). Uzziah also thought that he was entitled as king to
sacrifice to God in the temple.

The priests opposed him, warning him that he was acting
improperly.

> Then Uzziah became furious; and he had a censer in his hand
> to burn incense. And while he was angry with the priests, leprosy
> broke out on his forehead, before the priests in the house of the
> LORD, beside the incense altar (v. 19).

The king remained a leper until he died. In accordance with
Biblical law (Leviticus 13, 14), he was separated from other people
in a lifetime quarantine (v. 21).

What is the meaning of this passage? It is reasonably clear:
there is a fundamental separation between the ministry of civil
justice (sword) and the ministry of the sacraments. The church is
a lawfully covenanted institution, a separate jurisdiction from the
state.

The church's covenant parallels the basic covenant pattern in the Bible. First, *transcendence/immanence* (presence). The minister and elders represent God to the people and the people to God. God is present with His people in the church worship meetings, especially during the serving of the Lord's Supper (communion).

Second, there is *hierarchy*. Elders rule over deacons, and both rule through service over the members. The elders serve as an appeals court in church disputes (1 Corinthians 3).

Third, there is *ethics*. The church preaches the gospel, declaring God's law for every area of life. The church is a counsellor, as the Levites were, to other institutions.

Fourth, there is *judgment*. The church excommunicates—cuts off from communion—as a prelude to the final judgment of God (1 Corinthians 5).

Fifth, there is *continuity*. The church is a continuing institution over time, the place where parents and children gather. It provides continuity for families through the sacrament of baptism.

Naturally, we see a rival church in satanic cults, but more importantly, in humanism's self-proclaimed agency of salvation, the messianic state.

The state seeks to serve as the voice of God, or what is the same today, the voice of man in a world where no God is said to exist. This is why tyrannies insist on elections, and require all citizens to vote in these meaningless elections. "Vox populi, vox dei": the voice of the people is the voice of god—the god of humanism.

Second, the state establishes a bureaucratic hierarchy. This hierarchy tells people how they must live. It is a top-down hierarchy.

Third, the state announces laws—an endless stream of laws. In the United States, every day, the national government's bureaucracy prints the *Federal Register*, which is over 200 pages long, in three columns of small print, which announces the new rules and regulations for the day. Over 54,000 pages appear each year. Hardly anyone except specialized lawyers can even read these laws. (Most of God's laws for the civil government appear in Exodus 20-23 and Deuteronomy).

Fourth, the state asserts itself to be judge over every aspect of life, invading the church and the family with barely a thought of the consequences. In Mexico, for instance, the state owns every church building and its land, and any "house church" is illegal. Neighbors can report worship activities to the police, and if the house is not previously registered as a church, the state can legally confiscate it.

Fifth, the state seeks to control the future by controlling capital. It taxes inheritances. It establishes long-term debts, thereby destroying the independent futures of taxpayers. It decapitalizes Christians.

Silencing the Whole Counsel of God

That Marxism should be promoted in the name of Christianity is the supreme irony of the twentieth century. The church has had no greater enemy in its history. Yet we have seen this pattern before. The false prophets of ancient Israel frequently spoke in the name of the God of Israel. These were the prophets that the evil kings wanted to hear. Even when King Ahab knew that his court prophets were telling him what he wanted to hear, not what was really the word of God, he preferred them. When he was asked by King Jehoshaphat of Judah to call in a true priest, Micaiah, Ahab knew he would prophesy bad news. When Micaiah prophesied good news, Ahab rebuked him: "How many times shall I make you swear that you tell me nothing but the truth in the name of the Lord?" (2 Chronicles 18:15). He knew the true from the false prophets.

So fierce had Ahab's hostility been toward the word of God that Ahab's servant Obadiah had to hide a hundred prophets in caves in order to save their lives (1 Kings 18:13). It was only under extreme pressure — the drought and famine — that Elijah could get Ahab to consent to the showdown on Mount Carmel between himself and the 850 evil prophets.

General apostasy is always accompanied by tyranny. When the people of Israel in the era of the Judges would begin to worship the gods of Canaan or Philistia, God would deliver them into the hands of their enemies. God said, in effect: "So you like the gods of Philistia, do you? Very well, let Me show you what those gods are really like. I will deliver you into their jurisdiction for a few years."

There are those today within the church who tell us that Old Testament laws are inherently tyrannical. They tell us that the church can live under any system of political law in the world, and still survive. But one system of law is supposedly forever forbidden: Biblical law. That would be intolerable. That would mean that Christians were exercising dominion. The power religionists do not want to hear that; neither do the escape religionists.

What we learn in the Old Testament is just the opposite: tyranny was the product of every rival law system in the ancient world *except* Old Testament law. The God of the Bible is the God of liberation. His law therefore produces liberation. Yet the critics of the Old Testament law system claim that civil rule in terms of Old Testament law would produce tyranny.

We can see just how effective the humanists have been in persuading Christians to give up their heritage of liberty for a mess of bureaucratic pottage.

So whenever the church begins to declare God's holy standards of civil rule, the state is outraged. "How dare you! It is your job to keep the people quiet," says the present ruler. "It is not your job to speak out on political questions. They are of no concern to the church."

The revolutionaries are equally outraged. "It is your job to preach revolution, not reform," says the Marxist liberation theologian. "It is not your job to preach peaceful change, the reconstruction of society by the preaching of the gospel, and the decapitalization of the state. No, the goal is to capture the state, strengthen it, and make it even more powerful."

The escapists are also outraged. "Look, we come to church to have our spirits soothed. You keep bringing up unpleasant topics. There is nothing we can do about any of the world's problems outside the four walls of the sanctuary. Preach Jesus, and Him crucified—and be sure to leave Him hanging on the cross, where He belongs."

The preaching of the full-scale gospel scares those who believe in political salvation, as well as those who believe in irresponsible, world-denying salvation. The message of the Bible is simple in principle: *comprehensive redemption*. Everything is to be brought under the dominion of Jesus, through His people, who represent Him as ambassadors and judges on earth. Everything. This means that Christ redeemed (bought back) the whole world. It means that there is no neutrality between Christ and Satan. Christ's rule must be established over everything before He delivers the kingdom up to His Father (1 Corinthians 15:24).

Avoiding Pastoral Responsibilities

Christian rule means rule in terms of Biblical law by every Christian in his God-given area of responsibility: family, business, education, or wherever. To preach such a gospel, the pastors must possess a vision of dominion. They must understand the Bible so well that they can see how it applies in many different "secular" fields. This is why pastors as a group need to be involved in specialized study, so that they can preach and write with authority. Each pastor needs to know one or two "secular" fields to which the Bible speaks. He should be in contact with other Christians who understand their fields. Then he can bring this comprehensive understanding of the Bible into the pulpit. He can begin to motivate Christians to become dominion-oriented.

This is a large responsibility. Few pastors know where to begin. They fear making mistakes, speaking out where they have no competence. Very well; their job is to begin studying until they have more competence. But it is so easy to agree with the state—"Keep the church out of politics (and everything else)"—and to avoid viewing the Bible as the source of blueprints for many areas of life, that few pastors ever begin. They avoid preaching the whole counsel of God.

Humanism teaches that the God of the Bible and His Word are not relevant to anything outside of (maybe) family life. The pietists (escape religionists) agree with the humanists. The only way to answer their criticisms is to show that the Bible *is* relevant to every area of life. This takes hard work, careful study, and risk.

Persecution

The church comes under immediate attack and control the day that the Communist allies of the liberation theologians attain political or military power. The church is seen as one of the two enemy institutions to the state, the other being the family. But churches are far easier to control than families. There are fewer of them, their property is visible, and their leaders can be threatened.

There is little question that there are two major reasons why churches are not yet being persecuted in non-communist countries. First, because existing political rulers do not want to take the risk yet of pressuring the churches. Second, the messages that most pastors are delivering from the pulpits are no particular threat to the political rulers. In short, there are high costs and low benefits for political rulers who attempt to silence the churches. Most of them have already adopted self-policing methods. They avoid controversy.

Nevertheless, the existence of legally independent sources of authority within society is always a threat in principle to humanist civil rulers. Churches that preach the whole counsel of God can expect trouble from the civil magistrates eventually. What should they do to prepare for this day?

First, they must make full use of prayer. Prayer gives Christians access to God's holy sanctuary. Corporate prayer through the church offers added power: this is God's ordained monopoly of corporate worship. Paul tells us to pray for the civil government, that the church might have peace (1 Timothy 2:1-3).

Second, the Psalms offer examples of wrathful prayers. These are sometimes called *imprecatory* psalms. They pray down God's wrath on His enemies, who are the enemies of the church. Psalm 83 is a good example. Psalm 74 is another. These are supposed to be public prayers, meaning official prayers of the church. If the rulers refuse to do what is righteous, and they become a threat to public peace and public good, then they are the legitimate targets of imprecatory prayers. We ask God to reform them or remove them.

In other words, the prayers of the church are to offer rulers both rewards and punishments, carrots and sticks. The rulers should understand that it is best to have the churches of a nation on their side. This reduces the likelihood of persecution.

Sometimes, the situation may have deteriorated to such an extent that the church's officers fear praying hostile prayers in public. They should then meet privately and offer up prayers in the name of the people. The worse the external situation is, the more wrathful the prayers should become. God is asked to defend His good name by defending His bride, the church.

Protector of the Family

One of the functions of the church is to strengthen and defend families. This means that parents are to be encouraged to take up their responsibilities as teachers of their children. Parents are required to teach God's law, from morning to night (Deuteronomy 6:6-7). Some of them may not know God's law well enough. The church is to teach them.

If the state is the primary agency of education (as it is in all humanist societies), then parents must be encouraged to remove their children from state schools and enroll them in private Christian schools. If this is illegal, then the church must encourage parents to spend time with their children to help them unlearn the lies they have been told by the evolutionists and Marxists in the state schools. There is a battle going on for the minds of the next generation. The humanists want to steal the inheritance of the families by capturing the minds of those who will inherit.

The family is the primary agency of welfare. Sometimes families do a poor job in this task. As a secondary agency of welfare, the church moves in and offers minimal charity, so that a temporary crisis can be avoided (2 Corinthians 8). The church should not attempt to create permanent dependence. Its job is to build up independent, dominion-oriented members. Charity can serve as a psychological support, encouraging people to take risks for the sake of the future. The church represents God, who will not allow His people to starve. But charity can also serve as a psychological crutch, an excuse for not working. Paul forbids this:

> For even when we were with you, we commanded you this: if anyone will not work, neither shall he eat (2 Thessalonians 3:10).

To reduce the financial risks to church members, the deacons should see to it that every member buys basic insurance policies to protect his family, if such policies are available. Insurance is one of the greatest inventions of the modern world. It allows people to share risks in an economical fashion. Life insurance and accident insurance are very important. If necessary, the church can pay life insurance premiums, and name itself as the trustee beneficiary of life insurance policies, so that widows and children can be assured care if the husbands die. But husbands should be encouraged to buy annual renewable term life insurance: no savings program, just a simple "I die, and the company pays" kind of policy.

Authority in the Church

As we have already seen, the fundamental kind of human government is *self*-government. No institutional government can afford to police its members day and night. Thus, the goal of preaching should be to increase the self-government of the members. They must be taught to recognize which Biblical principle applies in each historical situation.

Self-government is to be invoked each time the church offers the Lord's Supper. "But let a man examine himself, and so let him eat of that bread and drink of that cup" (1 Corinthians 11:28). This involves self-examination and confession of sins before God. By having frequent communion meals, the church encourages self-government among members. This is a strong argument for having weekly communion. But church officers should be warned in advance: introducing weekly communion to a God-fearing church will often create major problems, including rebellion and church splits. There are wolves in sheep's clothing in every church, especially churches that have not had a continuing program of discipline through excommunication. The evil-doers in the congregation will feel the pressure of weekly communion. They will surface, and they usually like to drag other members into controversies against the church's officers. Be prepared for this. That is

what weekly communion is supposed to accomplish: to weed out
(Matthew 13:7, 22) those who resent God's discipline over them.
Weekly communion forces them to deal with this moral problem
every week.

Elders must begin to serve as appeals courts (1 Corinthians 6).
They must be ready to put a halt to all rumors and gossip. Continued tale-bearing is a sin (Leviticus 19:16). Every time a bad
report comes to a church elder, he should ask the tale-bearer to
repeat the accusation because the problem may get to the trial
stage. It would be wise for the officer to carry a little note pad for
this purpose. Just take it out, note the date, write down the tale-
bearer's name, and then ask him to repeat the accusation slowly.
This will reduce tale-bearing drastically. It forces the tale-bearer
to speak precisely. The cost of becoming a false witness (perjurer)
is to have the penalty that would have been imposed on the victim
imposed on the false witness (Deuteronomy 19:19).

By keeping disputes within the church out of the secular
courts, the state is kept at a greater distance. The state will be
more likely to recognize the church as an independent jurisdiction, which God says it is. To submit to the law of a rival god (humanism), church members have violated the covenant.

Any church member who appeals a decision of the church to
the state should be instantly excommunicated. He is thereby calling in the state to judge the church. This is an act of defiance.
Also, once he is excommunicated and is no longer to be regarded
as a Christian for institutional decision-making purposes (1 Corinthians 5), church members can then go into the secular courts to
challenge him and defend the church from his public accusations.
(The obvious example is a dispute concerning a church-granted
divorce, especially the accusation of adultery or other major sin
against one of the spouses. When the announcement of the
reasons for the excommunication and divorce are made public,
the guilty party may seek vengeance against the church.)

As is the case in every covenantal institution, judicial authority is lodged at the top (the principle of representation or presence), but the chain of command is to be imposed in a bottom-up

manner, not top-down. The appeals court, not the bureaucratic command system, is the Biblical model. The appeals court structure increases the degree of self-reliance and independent decision-making by Christians. It increases self-government under God. This increases the division of labor and specialization within the church (1 Corinthians 12), and therefore it increases the extent of the authority of Christians over the creation. Each member can better exercise his specific gifts before God and man.

Church Prerogatives

The church has a right to speak out on any issue that the Bible deals with. The church is not an agency of civil government, family government, or any other human government. It is the judge of all institutions before God, for it is the keeper of the keys of heaven (the sacraments), and it proclaims the word of God from the pulpit. Eventually, Christians will judge the angels (1 Corinthians 6:3).

The church should own its own property if it can afford to buy it in open free market competition. If the church is the highest bidder for a piece of property, and the seller wishes to sell to the church, then no other governmental agency should refuse to allow the sale.

The church must not be taxed by any agency of civil government. It is an independent legal jurisdiction in the eyes of God. The church is tax-immune in God's eyes. Any violation of this immunity is comparable to Uzziah's violation of the temple. The church should pray down God's wrath on the civil magistrates who made the decision to collect taxes from God's house.

If voluntary charitable donations are considered income tax deductible for donors by any level of civil government, then donors to the church should be entitled to take advantage of this special exemption.

The church is a separate legal entity. Its debts (if any) are not the personal debts of its individual members. The civil courts may convict church officers as criminals in their capacity as officers (for example, misappropriation of funds), and assess appropriate penalties against them personally or against the church's assets if the church's authority was misused by the officers to commit a crime, but these penalties are not the obligations of the members.

If churches set up schools, these schools must be legally independent of all state regulation except normal safety and health regulations that are applied equally to all public buildings, especially buildings owned by the state. There must be no interference with the curriculum materials of the church-run schools.

Summary

The church is structured along the lines of God's covenant. It is a separate legal jurisdiction in the eyes of God. It possesses the monopoly of the sacraments. Its authority to excommunicate is its chief power.

It speaks the whole counsel of God. *Nothing that the Bible addresses is outside the preaching jurisdiction of the church.* Any attempt to limit this preaching function represents an assault by God's enemies against the Word of God.

For society to receive the full blessings of God, individuals and other institutions must respect the lawful jurisdiction of the church. If the state hampers the church in its preaching, then God will bring judgment against the civil magistrates involved. If the whole population agrees that the state should hamper the church, then this spiritual sodomy will be punished by God covenantally, meaning collectively. The equivalent of fire and brimstone is imminent (Genesis 19). Individuals who wish to avoid such collective judgment would be wise to take up the church's cause.

In summary:

1. The king in ancient Israel was not allowed to exercise the priest's prerogative of making sacrifice to God.
2. The ministry of the sword is different from the ministry of the sacraments.
3. The church's covenantal structure parallels the general covenant structure.
4. Satan establishes a rival ecclesiastical structure through the state.

5. The satanic state seeks out false prophets.

6. General apostasy is always accompanied by tyranny.

7. Modern Christians believe that God's laws in the Old Testament would promote tyranny today.

8. Humanists argue the same way.

9. In the Old Testament, all other law structures promoted tyranny.

10. Established humanist civil governments, revolutionaries, and escape religionists all resent the church's preaching of the whole Bible.

11. Pastors fear adding to their responsibilities.

12. Preaching the whole counsel of God necessarily involves becoming familiar with many aspects of thought and culture.

13. The church comes under persecution when systematic, dedicated humanists come into political power.

14. The churches must pray: peace prayers and judgment prayers.

15. The church is the protector of the family.

16. The church is a secondary welfare agency, filling in where families fail.

17. Self-government is basic to a Biblical church.

18. Self-government is invoked before the Lord's Supper (self-examination, confession of sin).

19. Weekly communion meals increase the frequency of the need of formal self-government.

20. Church elders are to serve as appeals court judges.

21. Formal trials will reduce gossip in the church.

22. The church is a separate jurisdiction from the state.

23. This is why it needs its own autonomous courts under God.

24. Judicial authority is at the top, but the system is activated bottom-up.

25. The satanic structure is bureaucratic, with action initiated at the top and imposed on the lower rungs of the institution.

26. The church has basic prerogatives as a separate jurisdiction: freedom from interference by the state.

8

THE LIBERATION OF THE STATE

Listen now to my voice; I will give you counsel, and God will be with you: Stand before God for the people, so that you may bring the difficulties to God. And you shall teach them the statutes and the laws, and show them the way in which they must walk and the work they must do. Moreover you shall select from all the people able men, such as fear God, men of truth, hating covetousness; and place such over them to be rulers of thousands, rulers of hundreds, rulers of fifties, and rulers of tens. And let them judge the people at all times. Then it will be that every great matter they shall bring to you, but every small matter they themselves shall judge. So it will be easier for you, for they will bear the burden with you. If you do this thing, and God so commands you, then you will be able to endure, and all this people will also go to their place in peace (Exodus 18:19b-23).

This was the advice of Jethro, Moses' father-in-law, when he saw the lines of people in front of Moses' tent, all waiting for justice. At that point in Israel's history, God gave them perfect justice directly, but not everyone had access to it. It took standing in long lines to get it. Moses grew weary, and the people grew weary waiting for judgment.

The Bible is not a perfectionist document. While it lays down a standard of human perfection (Genesis 17:1; 1 Kings 8:61; Matthew 5:48)—a standard met only by Jesus Christ (Matthew 3:17; Romans 3:23; 2 Corinthians 5:21)—it nonetheless acknowledges in its very law code that the administration of even a perfect law system designed by God must be understood as fallible, limited, and tainted with sin. As this passage amply demonstrates, the Bible is hostile to the humanists' quest for perfect justice on earth. There will eventually be perfect justice administered by God on judgment day.

Under Moses' direct rule, God's revelation was instantly available in any given case. Yet there was insufficient time available for Moses to hear every case of legal dispute in the land. Perfect justice was limited by time and space. Men had to come to Moses' tent and stand in (presumably) long lines (Exodus 18:14). The quest for perfect earthly justice from God through His servant Moses was eating up countless man-hours. Not only was Moses' time limited, but so was the time of those who stood in lines.

When people are waiting for justice, their lives tend to come to a halt. They become unproductive. They are afraid to commit scarce economic resources to their tasks. They hold back, hoping to get an area of uncertainty in their lives resolved by civil justice.

Jethro recognized the limitations of even a system of perfect justice, where God's word came directly to the people. Such a system could not work. It was too great a burden. Better to have an appeals court system judged by men with less than perfect insight, so long as justice was speedy. Better to have speedy justice and to get back to living normal routines than to have perfect justice several years down the road of life.

Who was fit to be a judge? The standards are similar (though not so rigorous) to the standards given for elders and deacons in the church (1 Timothy 3): ". . . able men, such as fear God, men of truth, hating covetousness." *Character* counts for more than technical knowledge of the law.

Consider the available judges. They had grown up as slaves. The whole generation, except for Joshua and Caleb, possessed slave mentalities. Nevertheless, their rule was preferable in most cases to a system which offered perfect justice in individual cases, but which had to ration the number of cases. Conclusion: *regular* and *predictable* justice provided by *responsible amateurs* is better than perfect justice provided on a sporadic or "first in line" basis. The burden of dispensing justice had to be shared (v. 22). This was required in order to permit the people to endure, going their way in peace (v. 23).

There were a lot of judges, too. Rashi, one of the most famous rabbis in Jewish history, estimated that there must have been at least 82,000 judges, or some 15% of the adult male population of 600,000. They were not all graduates of state-accredited law schools!

The Covenantal Structure of Civil Government

First, there is *transcendence/immanence* (presence). Moses serves as the representative of the people before God. "Stand before God for the people. . . ." He is not a representative of the people to the people, but rather to God.

Second, Moses heads up a *hierarchical* system of law courts. He is at the top of an appeals court pyramid. He is held accountable by God.

Third, he speaks the *law of God*. He sets forth the general principles and goals of a godly society. "And you shall teach them the statutes and the laws, and show them the way in which they must walk and the work they must do."

Fourth, he issues *judgment*. "Then it will be that every great matter they shall bring to you. . . ." He compares the people's actions with the general standards of God's law, and he renders judgment concerning who is responsible for what.

Fifth, there is *continuity*. "And let them judge the people at all times." Through time, this system allows men to seek justice continually. There is never to be a period in which God's law is not being enforced. "If you do this thing, and God so commands you, then you will be able to endure, and all this people will also go to their place in peace."

Satan's Version

Satan offers his version of the civil covenant. It is similar to God's, yet ethically opposite.

First, there is *no true transcendence or presence*. The representative of the people represents something other than God: the Party, the will of the people as a collective, the forces of history, the Volk, the nation, the spirit of the age, etc. But he does not represent a sovereign God to the people, or the people to a sovereign God.

Second, there is *hierarchy*. A top-down system of bureaucratic rule is established. It is not a bottom-up system of appeals courts, with a large degree of personal initiative, responsibility, and freedom at the lower levels. The emphasis is on the omniscience of the state, computerized planning, massive statistics, and central management of all of life.

Third, there are *laws* — myriads of laws. These laws are so numerous and so complex that only bureaucrats who make it their lives to know the rules, and lawyers who get paid to interpret them, can understand them. This leads to elitism. Also, these laws are constantly being rewritten: evolutionary justice in a world of shifting principles.

Fourth, there is *judgment*. The state possesses almost unlimited powers of executing judgment. An ever-growing army of enforcers announce arbitrary judgments that increase the power of the state.

Fifth, there is an *attempted continuity* through taxes and confiscation. Rising taxes weaken all other institutions and strengthen the hand of the state. Yet God's people today do not seem to understand the extent of their bondage.

The Right of Appeal

In the Bible, the right of appeal was limited to "great matters." Cases involving fundamental principle, and those that would be likely to have important repercussions throughout the society, were the ones that were to be sent up the judicial chain of appeals. In order to limit the number of cases being sent to Moses for a final decision, the judges at each level must have had the right to refuse to reconsider the verdict of a lower court. If the judge did not believe that the decision of the lower court was in error, and if the higher court decided that the case was of relatively little importance as a precedent for society at large, the case was settled. Access to Moses' supreme court was restricted to great cases, and this required screening by the lower courts. Jethro understood that the limitations on Moses' time were paralyzing the justice system. Obviously, if every case considered by the lower courts eventually wound up in front of Moses, the hierarchy of courts would have provided no respite for Moses. The screening feature of the court system was fundamental to its success. This meant that the majority of litigants had to content themselves with something less than perfect justice.

Jethro understood that *endless litigation threatens the survival of the system of justice.* Losers in a case clearly have an incentive to appeal, if the possibility of overturning the decision of the lower court judge offers hope. So there has to be restraint on the part of higher court judges to refrain from constant overturning of lower court decisions. Furthermore, a society composed of people who always are going to court against each other will suffer from clogged courts and delayed justice. A society, in short, which is not governed by *self-restrained people*, and which does not provide other means of settling disputes besides the civil government — church courts, arbitration panels, mediation boards, industry-wide courts, and so forth — will find itself paralyzed.

Breakdown of the U.S. Court System

Macklin Fleming is a justice of the California Court of Appeal. His book, *The Price of Perfect Justice* (Basic Books, 1974), documents the increasing paralysis of the legal system in the United States. It is this *quest for earthly perfection* — a messianic, God-imitating quest — that has been the U.S. legal system's undoing.

> The fuel that powers the modern legal engine is the ideal of perfectability — the concept that with the expenditure of sufficient time, patience, energy, and money it is possible eventually to achieve perfect justice in all legal process. For the past twenty years this ideal has dominated legal thought, and the ideal has been widely translated into legal action. Yet a look at almost any specific area of the judicial process will disclose that the noble ideal has consistently spawned results that can only be described as

pandemoniac. For example, in criminal prosecutions we find as long as five months spent in the selection of a jury; the same murder charge tried five different times; the same issues of search and seizure reviewed over and over again, conceivably as many as twenty-six different times; prosecutions pending a decade or more; accusations routinely sidestepped by an accused who makes the legal machinery the target instead of his own conduct (p. 3).

Where have modern secular humanistic courts failed? Fleming cites Lord Macauley's rule: the government that attempts more than it ought ends up doing less that it should. Human law has its limits. Human courts have their limits.

The law cannot be both infinitely just and infinitely merciful; nor can it achieve both perfect form and perfect substance. These limitations were well understood in the past. But today's dominant legal theorists, impatient with selective goals, with limited objectives, and with human fallibility, have embarked on a quest for perfection in all aspects of the social order, and, in particular, perfection in legal procedure (p. 4).

The requirements of legal perfection, Fleming says, involve the following hypothetical conditions: totally impartial and competent tribunals, unlimited time for the defense, total factuality, total familiarity with the law, the abolition of procedural error, and the denial of the use of disreputable informants, despite the fact, as he notes, that "the strongest protection against organized thievery lies in the fact that thieves sell each other out" (p. 5). The defenders of costless justice have adopted the slogan, "Better to free a hundred guilty men than to convict a single innocent man." But what about the costs to future victims of the hundred guilty men? The legal perfectionists refuse to count the costs of their hypothetical universe (p. 6).

The whole system procrastinates: judges, defense lawyers, prosecutors, appeals courts, even the stenographic corps (p. 71). Speedy justice is no longer a reality. Prisoners appeal constantly to federal courts on the basis of *habeas corpus*: illegal detention because of an unconstitutional act on the part of someone, anyone. In 1940, 89 prisoners convicted in state courts made such an appeal. In 1970, the figure was 12,000 (p. 27). Thus, concludes Fleming:

> The consequence of this expansion of federal power over state criminal procedure through the creation of fiat prohibitions and rigidly ritualistic rules has been to elevate formalism to constitutional right, to complicate every significant phase of criminal procedure to the point where in some instances the system of criminal law has difficulty functioning and in others it turns loose persons who are patently guilty (p. 97).

Salvation by Law

The quest for perfect justice leads inevitably to *arbitrary jurisprudence* and *public lawlessness*. Joseph in Pharaoh's jail, Daniel in the lions' den, and Jesus on the cross all testify to the imperfections in human courts of law. Nevertheless, godly men can live with imperfect justice, just as they live with imperfections in all other spheres of human life, because they know that perfect justice *does* exist and will be made manifest on the day of judgment.

Life is too short to demand perfect justice on earth; better by far to have speedy justice handed down by godly amateurs than to suffer with the clogged courts of messianic humanism. We need not wring our hands in despair because men's courts, in time and on earth, fail to meet the standards of perfection which will reign supreme in God's court. We are not saved either by the perfect spirit of the law or the perfect letter of the law. We are surely not saved by imperfect imitations of the spirit and letter of the law. We are not saved by law.

Salvation by law is an ancient heresy, and it leads to the triumph of statist theology. Christianity is in total opposition to this doctrine. As R. J. Rushdoony writes in his book, *Politics of Guilt and Pity* (Craig Press, 1970):

> The reality of man apart from Christ is guilt and masochism. And guilt and masochism involve an unshakable inner slavery which governs the total life of the non-Christian. The politics of the anti-Christian will thus inescapably be *the politics of guilt*. In the politics of guilt, man is perpetually drained in his social energy and

cultural activity by his overriding sense of guilt and his masochistic activity. He will progressively demand of the state a redemptive role. What he cannot do personally, i.e., to save himself, he demands that the state do for him, so that the state, as man enlarged, becomes the human savior of man. The politics of guilt, therefore, is not directed, as the Christian politics of liberty, to the creation of godly justice and order, but to the creation of a redeeming order, a saving state (p. 9).

Christian jurisprudence cannot adopt a doctrine of the saving state and remain orthodox. The adoption of just such a concept of the state in the twentieth century testifies to the extent to which the modern world has abandoned Christian orthodoxy.

Jamming the System

One of the most important aspects of any legal order is the willingness of the citizens of a society to exercise self-restraint. This means that men must emphasize *self-government*, as well as gain access to court systems that serve as alternatives to civil government. This was a basic feature of the Western legal tradition after the mid-twelfth century, although since World War I, the rise of socialistic administrative states has begun to undermine this tradition, according to Professor Harold Berman of Harvard in his important book, *Law and Revolution* (Harvard University Press, 1983). He says that this development now threatens the survival of freedom in the West.

Self-government is not a zero-price resource. The emphasis in the Bible on training up children in the details of Biblical law must be understood as a requirement of citizens to provide "social overhead capital" for civilization: respect for law and therefore self-restraint. Another aspect of the public's respect for civil law is the *self-restraint of government officials* in not burdening the society with a massive, incomprehensible structure of administrative law.

When civil law reaches into every aspect of the daily lives of men, the state loses a very important *subsidy* from the public, namely, men's willingness to submit voluntarily to the civil law. Any legal structure is vulnerable to the foot-dragging of the public. If men refuse to submit to regulations that cannot be enforced, one by one, by the legal system, then that system will be destroyed. Court-jamming will paralyze it. This is a familiar phenomenon in the United States in the final decades of the twentieth century.

It is possible to bring down any legal system simply by taking advantage of every legal avenue of delay. Any administrative system has procedural rules; by following these rules so closely that action on the part of the authorities becomes hopelessly bogged down in red tape (procedural details), the protestors can paralyze the system. Too many laws can produce lawlessness. The courts can no longer enforce their will on the citizens. At the same time, administrative agencies can destroy individual citizens, knowing that citizens must wait too long to receive justice in the courts. The result is a combination of anarchy and tyranny: the antinomian legacy.

Recognizing Our Limitations

What we can and should strive for is to conform our human law codes to the explicit requirements of the Ten Commandments and the case-law applications of Biblical law. The answer to our legal crisis is not to be found in the hypothetical perfection of formal law, nor can it be found in the hypothetical perfection of substantive (ethical) justice. Judges will make errors, but these errors can be minimized by placing them within the framework of Biblical law. Before God gave the nation of Israel a comprehensive system of law, Jethro gave Israel a comprehensive system of decentralized courts. By admitting the impossibility of the goal for earthly perfect justice, Moses made possible the reign of imperfectly applied revealed law: perfect in principle, but inevitably flawed in application. The messianic goal of a perfect law-order, in time and on earth, was denied to Moses and his successors.

One of the most obvious failures of the modern administrative civil government system is its quest for perfect justice and perfect control over the details of economic life. The implicit assertion of omniscience on the part of the central planners is economically fatal. The result of such an assertion is an increase of regulations, increased confusion among both rulers and ruled, and a growing disrespect for civil law. The productivity of the West cannot be maintained in the face of such an exponential build-up of central power. It is only because the laws are not consistent, nor universally enforced or obeyed, that the modern messianic state has survived. The price of perfect human justice is too high to be achieved by the efforts of men.

Theft By Ballot Box

The Bible says it is immoral to covet your neighbor's goods (Exodus 20:17). Yet modern socialist societies legislate covetousness, promote it, and survive in terms of it. They teach people that the commandment against theft should read, "You shall not steal, except by majority vote." This is the heart and soul of Marxism's liberation theology.

The commandment against covetousness refers to an individual who looks longingly at his neighbor's property. *The beginning of covetousness is clearly the human heart.* Men want goods that they have neither earned nor inherited. Their relationships with their neighbors cannot possibly be in conformity to God's law when such feelings are present in their hearts. The fact that one man possesses goods that are confiscatable in the eyes of his neighbor will disrupt their relationship. The possessor will be seen by the covetous man as an illegitimate owner, someone who has no right, under God, to maintain control over his possessions.

The commandment has implications beyond the local neighborhood. *When covetousness becomes widespread, the next step is political coercion.* The very usage of the words, "to covet," implies violence. The covetous man will not limit his attempt to gain control of another man's property to an offer to purchase. Like Ahab, who was determined to gain control of Naboth's vineyard when Naboth refused to sell, the covetous man seeks to coerce his neighbor. When this cannot be done with the connivance of the police — outright oppression or theft — then he seeks to gain control of the civil government.

Covetous men can join forces and encourage the civil government to adopt policies of wealth redistribution. The *monopoly of legal violence* possessed by the civil government can then be turned against property owners. Those within the civil government can gain control over people's assets. They can then use them personally, or inside a government bureau, or distribute them to political special-interest groups. Political covetousness is a manifestation of *unrestrained desire* and the *threat of violence.*

When the civil government becomes an instrument of covetousness, its monopoly of violence increases the danger of theft. A new commandment is adopted: "Thou shalt not covet, except by majority vote." What private citizen can effectively defend his property against unjust magistrates? Naboth died in his attempt to keep that which was his by law — God's law.

The misuse of the civil government in this way is doubly evil. First, it violates the principle of responsible stewardship. Second, it misuses the office of magistrate. *The spread of covetousness cannot be restrained by the magistrate when the structure of civil government is deeply influenced by political covetousness.* The old warning against putting the foxes in charge of the chicken coop is accurate: when the state becomes the agent of widespread covetousness, the whole society is threatened. *Waves of power-struggles ensue, for each special-interest group recognizes that it must gain control of the primary agency of wealth redistribution.* The more power is offered to the controllers by means of statist coercive mechanisms, the more ferocious is the struggle to gain access to the seats of power.

The covetous person resents his own station in life. Someone else possesses what he wants. He is dissatisfied with the role he is playing in God's plan for the ages. It is this resentment against one's station in life which Paul condemns (1 Corinthians 7:21-22). One person desires another's good looks, prestige, or worldly possessions. He feels thwarted by his own limitations, and therefore thwarted by his environment. God has thwarted his personal development, the covetous man is asserting. The Bible teaches that the other person is working out his salvation or damnation before God. His property must be respected. Nevertheless, the covetous man thinks that he can appropriate for himself the fruits of the other man's labor, as if those fruits were unrelated to that man's personal responsibility before God as a steward.

Totalitarianism vs. the Tithe

Totalitarian societies develop from the attempt of socialist planners to mold the economy into a centrally directed framework. Nothing must deviate from the central economic plan, since human freedom will thwart any such plan. Thus, the power to redistribute wealth in accordance with some preconceived statist program eventually destroys human freedom and therefore thwarts responsibility to act as a steward under God. *Covetousness, when legislated, becomes a major foundation of totalitarianism.*

The civil government is to be restrained by Biblical law. The warning of Samuel against the establishment of a human kingship stands as a classic statement of what earthly kingdoms involve. The king will draft sons to serve in his armed forces. He will conscript daughters to serve as cooks and confectioners. He will confiscate the best agricultural land. He will impose a tithe on the flocks. In short, the king will collect a tithe for himself (1 Samuel 8:11-19). The Hebrew state, Samuel promised, will be such a burden on them that they will cry out to God to deliver them, but He will not do it (v. 18). By denying God and His law-order, the Hebrews placed themselves under the sovereignty of man, and this sovereignty was centralized in the civil government. It is an ungodly state which demands tax payments as large as ten percent, God's tithe. How much worse is a state that requires more than God's tithe. Such a state has elevated itself to the position of a god. It is a false god. It is demonic.

Social Cooperation

When men do not trust their neighbors, it becomes expensive for them to cooperate in projects that would otherwise be mutually beneficial to them. They hesitate to share their goals, feelings, and economic expectations with each other. After all, if a man is known to be economically successful in a covetous society, he faces the threat of theft, either by individuals or bureaucrats. He faces the hostility of his associates. He faces others on a regular basis who are determined to confiscate what he has. The obvious response is to conceal one's success from others. But this also means concealing one's economic expectations.

Planning becomes clothed in secrecy. The planning agency of the family limits its goals. Disputes between families increase, since families cannot easily cooperate under such circumstances. The future is a topic of discussion only in vague terms, except in the privacy of family economic planning councils. The social division of labor is thwarted, and the future-orientation of communities is drastically reduced, since men refuse to discuss plans openly.

God forbids theft; covetousness is the *inward desire* that leads to theft or fraud. It is the evil desire which overwhelms the law's restraint on the sinner, the desire to have another man's property, whether or not the other man benefits from the transaction.

Voluntary exchange offers the other man an opportunity. He may not have known of the opportunity. He may not have known of a person's willingness to part with some resource in order to obtain what he, the owner, possesses. It is not immoral to offer another person an opportunity, unless the opportunity is innately immoral (such as offering to buy his wife's favors). *Covetousness is the lawless desire to take the other man's property, whether or not he finds the transaction beneficial.* When covetousness is common, men lose faith in their neighbors, in the social and political structure which protects private property, and in the benefits offered by the division of labor. Covetousness threatens the very fabric of society.

The tenth commandment was given to us so that we might enjoy the fruits of *social peace* and *social cooperation.* This is equally true of the earlier commandments. The law-order of the Bible is a means of *reducing conflict* and *extending the division of labor.* Greater efficiency becomes possible through the division of labor. Whatever contributes to social peace thereby tends to increase per capita productivity, and therefore per capita income. People have an economic incentive to cooperate. The prohibition against covetousness increases social cooperation by reducing its costs.

It is significant that the prohibition begins with the mind of man. There is no means of enforcing any civil law against thoughts, but God's law applies to men's thoughts. Since the very concept of covetousness involves the threat of violence and oppression, the *outworkings of covetousness* can be controlled by civil law, assuming the civil government has not been corrupted by a philosophy of universal legislated covetousness. The costs of policing the visible manifestations of covetousness are high. By focusing on the hearts of men, the Bible reduces the costs of law enforcement.

Men are to be taught from an early age that covetousness is a sin against God. These instruction costs are to be borne initially by the family (Deuteronomy 6:7). By making men aware of God's hostility to covetousness, teachers of the law reduce the need for heavy taxation, either for law enforcement against visible, coercive oppressors, or for programs of legislated covetousness, i.e., "social welfare" programs. By helping to increase the social division of labor, the *internalization of the law against covetousness* helps to increase per capita output, also reducing thereby the proportion of income going to support law enforcement. The society is blessed in two ways: reduced crime (including the crime of statist wealth redistribution programs) and increased output per capita. *Men wind up with more wealth after taxes. They increase their opportunities for responsible action before God and man.*

As always, good government must always begin with self-government under God's law.

Summary

Social peace is the goal — the social peace demanded by the prophet Isaiah: "They shall not hurt nor destroy in all My holy mountain: for the earth shall be full of the knowledge of the LORD, as the waters cover the sea" (Isaiah 11:9). *The juridical foundation of such peace is Biblical law.* The Ten Commandments serve as the basis of long-term, God-blessed social peace.

One important aspect of Biblical social peace is the *absence of covetousness*— in the hearts of men, in the relationships between neighbors, and in the legislation of civil governments. Where cov-

etousness reigns, there can be no social peace. There also cannot
be personal freedom.

The Marxist theory that all progress comes through class
struggle and revolutionary violence is an evil theory. The Bible
teaches that progress comes through the extension of God's laws
into every area of life. The war between good and evil is ethical. It
is not a class war.

Our political goal should be to create *a covenantal system of civil
law,* from local government to a highly limited central government. This process of bringing civil government under God's law
must begin with self-government. It must be a *bottom-up* process.
Any attempt to impose a system of Biblical civil freedom on a society which is satanic or humanist at its religious core will prove to
be unsuccessful. Our goal is revolution, but not violent revolution. Our goal is a revolution in the souls of men, passing from
death to life. Our civil institutions should progressively reflect the
transition from death to life.

In summary:

1. The Bible does not teach that human courts can ever provide perfect justice.

2. Speedy justice is more important than perfect justice, even
if perfect justice were available.

3. The Bible recommends an appeals court system.

4. The judges are to be moral men, not necessarily legal tech-
nicians.

5. Biblical civil government has the same five-part structure as
God's covenant.

6. Satan's imitation also has five parts.

7. Endless court cases threaten the productivity of society.

8. Men must be willing to suffer small injustices for the sake of
getting on with life.

9. The quest for perfect justice is beginning to destroy modern
courts.

10. The Bible rejects the pagan idea of salvation by law.

11. The state is not an agency of salvation.

12. Both citizens and civil magistrates must exercise self-
restraint.

13. We are limited creatures and must acknowledge this in our civil institutions.

14. We must not use the state as an agency of plunder.

15. When the state becomes an agency of plunder, evil men seek to capture the state.

16. The state is not entitled to even as much as a tithe: ten percent of income.

17. We want social cooperation and peace.

18. Socialism reduces social cooperation and peace.

19. The Christian goal is social peace.

9

THE LIBERATION OF THE ECONOMY

You shall not steal (Exodus 20:15).

The economy is *not* a covenant institution. It does *not* require the swearing of a self-maledictory oath, nor are such oaths allowable in business dealings.[1] The economy is primarily an outgrowth of the family, though unmarried persons can of course participate. The modern form of ownership, the corporation, is a business extension of the church: the owners of the corporation, like members of a church, are not personally liable for the debts of the organization.

Why include a chapter on the economy in a book on liberation theology? Because the Marxist liberation theologians have made economics the most important aspect of their theology. They follow Marx, who made the economic mode of production the bedrock foundation of all society and of all social analysis. The Marxist liberation theologians hate the free market. They hate self-government. They promote the satanic system of top-down bureaucratic management by an elite of central planners. Thus, their views on the economy are as satanic and as dangerous as their views on the individual, the family, the church, and the state.

The Prohibition Against Theft

It has long been recognized by Christian commentators that the Biblical case for private property rests more heavily on the

---

1. Gary North, *The Sinai Strategy: Economics and the Ten Commandments* (Tyler, Texas: Institute for Christian Economics, 1986), ch. 3.

passage cited at the beginning this chapter—the eighth command-ment—than on any other passage in the Bible. Individuals are prohibited by Biblical law from forcibly appropriating the fruits of another man's labor, or his inheritance. The civil government is required by the Bible to defend a social order based on the rights of private ownership. The various laws requiring restitution that are found in Exodus 22 explicitly limit the state in its imposition of sanctions against thieves, but there can be no doubt that it is the civil government which is required to impose them.

Rights of ownership mean that God transfers to specific men and organizations the sole and exclusive ability to use specific property for certain kinds of ends, and the state is to *exclude* others from the unauthorized use of such property. Property *rights* there-fore refer to *legal immunities* from interference by others in the ad-ministration of property. The duties associated with dominion are more readily and effectively achieved by individuals and societies through adherence to the private property system, which is one reason why the Bible protects private ownership. *Private property is basic to effective dominion.*

The only conceivable Biblical argument against this inter-pretation of the commandment against theft would be an asser-tion that the only valid form of ownership is ownership by the state, meaning control by bureaucracies established by civil law. But to argue along these lines demands evidence that the Bible, both Old Testament and New Testament, authorized the public (state) ownership of all goods. There is not a shred of evidence for such a view, and massive evidence against it. The tenth com-mandment prohibits coveting the property of a *neighbor*, which is plain enough. The Biblical social order is a social order which acknowledges and defends the rights of private property. This prohibition binds individuals and institutions, including the state.

God Owns the World

The foundation of property rights is ultimate ownership of all things by God, the Creator. God owns the whole world.

For every beast of the forest is Mine, and the cattle on a thousand hills. I know all the birds of the mountains: and the wild beasts of the field are Mine. If I were hungry, I would not tell you: for the world is Mine, and all its fullness (Psalm 50:10-12).

God's sovereignty is absolute. The Biblical concept of property rests on this definition of God's authority over the creation. The Bible provides us with data concerning God's delegation of responsibility to men as individuals and as members of collective associations, but all human sovereignty, including property rights, must be understood as *limited, delegated, and covenantal* in nature.

Christ's parable of the talents presents the sovereignty of God in terms of an analogy of a *loan* from a lord to his servants. The servants have an obligation to increase the value of capital entrusted to them. They are directly responsible to their lord, who is the real owner of the capital. *Ownership* is therefore *stewardship*. Men's rights of ownership are delegated, covenantal rights. God's "loan" must be repaid with capital gains, or at the very least, with interest (Matthew 25:27).

Each person is fully responsible before God for the lawful and profitable administration of God's capital, which includes both spiritual capital and economic capital (Luke 12:48). This is one of Christ's "pocketbook parables," and while it was designed to illustrate God's absolute sovereignty over the affairs of men, it nevertheless conveys a secondary meaning, namely, the legitimate rights of private ownership.

God distributed to Adam and Eve the resources of the world. They were made covenantally responsible for the care and expansion of this capital base when God established His dominion covenant with them. This same covenant was reestablished with Noah and his family (Genesis 9:1-7). In the originally sinless condition of Adam and Eve, this initial distribution of the earth's resources could be made by God in terms of an *original harmony of man's interests*.

This harmony included *hierarchy*, for Eve was functionally subordinate to Adam (though not ethically inferior). The God-designed harmony of interests was never an equalitarian relationship. It is not equalitarian in the post-Fall world. The church, as the body of Christ, is similarly described in terms of an organic unity which is supposed to be harmonious, with each "organ" essential to the proper functioning of the whole, yet with each performing separate tasks (1 Corinthians 12). All are under Christ, the head of the church (Ephesians 5:23).

God's universe is orderly. *There is a God-ordained regularity in economic affairs.* There is a predictable, lawful relationship between personal industriousness and wealth, between laziness and poverty.

> How long will you slumber, O sluggard? When will you rise from your sleep? A little sleep, a little slumber, a little folding of the hands to sleep—So shall your poverty come on you like a robber, and your need like an armed man (Proverbs 6:9-11).

> Wealth gained by dishonesty will be diminished: but he that gathers by labor will increase (Proverbs 13:11).

This applies to individuals, families, corporations, and nations. Not every godly man or organization will inevitably prosper economically, in time and on earth, and not every evil man will lose his wealth during his lifetime (Luke 16:19-31), but in the aggregate, there will be a significant correlation between *covenantal faithfulness* and *external prosperity*. In the long run, the wealth of the wicked is laid up for the just (Proverbs 13:22). This same principle applies to national, cultural, and racial groups (Deuteronomy 8). Long-term poverty in a society is a sign of God's judgment.

Covenantal law governs the sphere of economics. Wealth flows to those who work hard, deal honestly with their customers, and honor God. To argue, as the Marxists and socialists do, that wealth flows in a free market social order towards those who are ruthless, dishonest, and blinded by greed, is to deny the Bible's explicit teachings concerning the nature of economic life. It is a denial of the covenantal lawfulness of the creation.

The Theology of Socialism

Critics of the free market system have inflicted great damage on those societies that have accepted such criticisms as valid. Men have concluded that the private property system is rigged against

the poor and weak, forcing them into positions of permanent servitude. Historically, on the contrary, *no social order has provided more
opportunities for upward social mobility than the free market.*

The remarkable advance of numerous immigrant groups, but
especially of Eastern European Jews, in the United States from
1880 to 1950, is historically unprecedented.[2] Today, the policies of
the socialist welfare state are making lifetime dependents out of a
substantial minority of citizens. The modern welfare system is
deeply flawed, not simply because it uses coercion to take income
from the employed, but because it destroys the will of the recipients to escape from the welfare system.

The politics of welfare is also leading to class conflict. George
Gilder's words in *Wealth and Poverty* are eloquent in this regard:

> A program to lift by transfers and preferences the incomes of
> less diligent groups is politically divisive—and very unlikely—
> because it incurs the bitter resistance of the real working class. In
> addition, such an effort breaks the psychological link between
> effort and reward, which is crucial to long-run upward mobility.
> Because effective work consists not in merely fulfilling the require-
> ments of labor contracts, but in "putting out" with alertness and
> emotional commitment, workers have to understand and feel
> deeply that what they are given depends on what they give—that
> they must supply work in order to demand goods. Parents and
> schools must inculcate this idea in their children both by instruc-
> tion and example. Nothing is more deadly to achievement than the
> belief that effort will not be rewarded, that the world is a bleak and
> discriminatory place in which only the predatory and the specially
> preferred can get ahead. Such a view in the home discourages the
> work effort in school that shapes earnings capacity afterward. As
> with so many aspects of human performance, work effort begins in
> family experiences, and its sources can be best explored through
> an examination of family structure. Indeed, after work the second
> principle of upward mobility is the maintenance of monogamous
> marriage and family.[3]

---

2. Thomas Sowell, *Race and Economics* (New York: David McKay Co., 1975),
Pt. II.

3. George Gilder, *Wealth and Poverty* (New York: Basic Books, 1981), pp. 68-69.

The Biblical perspective on marriage, like the Biblical perspective on the foundations of economic growth, points to both ideas: the relationship between *work and reward*, and the central importance of the *family bond*. Men are told to have faith in the work-reward relationship, which encourages them to take risks and invest time and effort to improving their own personal work habits.

The Bible tells us that such efforts will not go unrewarded, whether on earth or in heaven (1 Corinthians 3). The habits of discipline, thrift, long hours of effort, investment in work skills, and the instruction of children in this philosophy of life will not be wasted, will not be "capital down the drain." On the contrary, the Bible teaches that *such an approach to life is the very essence of the dominion covenant.* Therefore, when philosophies contrary to the philosophy of Biblical accumulation and dominion are encountered, Christians should recognize them for what they are.

When men are taught that the capitalist (free market, meaning voluntary exchange) system is rigged against them, that they have a legal and moral right to welfare payments, and that those who live well as a result of their own labor, effort, and forecasting skills are immoral and owe the bulk of their wealth to the poor, we must recognize the source of these teachings: the pits of hell. This is Satan's counter-philosophy, which is expressly intended to thwart godly men in their efforts to subdue the earth to the glory of God.

This radically anti-Biblical philosophy is not simply a matter of intellectual error; it is *a conscious philosophy of destruction,* a systematically anti-Biblical framework which is calculated to undercut successful Christians by means of false guilt and paralysis. That such teachings are popular among Christian intellectuals in the latter years of the twentieth century only testifies to their abysmal ignorance—indeed, their judicial blindness (Matthew 3:14-15)—concerning Biblical ethics and economic theory. Christians have adopted the politics of envy from the secular humanists, especially in college and seminary classrooms. We live in an age of guilt-manipulators, and some of them use Scripture to their evil ends.

Liberating Planet Earth

Property and Democracy

The commandment against theft does not read: "You shall not steal, except by majority vote." We need to have private property rights respected not just by criminals, but also by individual citizens who find that they can extract wealth from others by means of state power. Furthermore, private property rights must be respected by profit-seeking businesses that would otherwise petition the state for economic assistance: tariffs, import quotas, below-market interest rate government loans, and so forth. To violate this principle is to call for the so-called "corporate state," another form of the welfare state — fascism, monopoly capitalism, or whatever. Whenever such a system has been constructed, it has led to reduced productivity and an increase in bureaucracy. The politicians are simply not competent enough to plan for an entire economy. To promote such a system of state planning and protection of industry is an illegitimate use of the ballot box, meaning democratic pressure politics.

Let us consider an example which has been debated from the Puritan revolution of the 1640's until today: *the property qualification for voting.* In the 1640's, the English Puritan military leader Oliver Cromwell led his forces to victory over the King, Charles the First. At the Putney Debates of Cromwell's New Model Army in 1647, Ireton, Cromwell's son-in-law, debated Rainsborough, the representative of the democratic faction, the Levellers. (The Levellers were not communists, but they were committed to a far wider franchise. The communists in the English Revolution were the Diggers, who called themselves the "True Levellers.")

Rainsborough argued that since all men are under the laws of a nation, they deserve a voice in the affairs of civil government. Ireton countered with a ringing defense of property rights. A man must have some stake in society, meaning property to defend, if he is to be entrusted with the right to vote. Men without permanent interests in the society — property, in other words — are too dangerous when handed the power of civil government. The property qualification is crucial to preserve society in a democratic order. "And if we shall go to take away this, we shall plainly go to take away all property and interest that any man hath either in land by inheritance, or in estate by possession, or in anything else. . . ."[4]

Two centuries later, Karl Marx concluded much the same, except that he favored the abolition of the property qualification for voting, precisely *because* it would destroy private property: ". . . the state as a state abolishes *private property* (i.e., man decrees by *political* means the *abolition* of private property) when it abolishes the *property* qualification for electors and representatives. . . . Is not private property ideally abolished when the non-owner comes to legislate for the owner of property? The *property qualification* is the last political form in which property is recognized."[5]

Democracy would be safe if men understood that it is immoral to vote other people's wealth into their pockets, *and if they obeyed the commandment not to steal.* There will come a day when the law of God that is in the hearts of Christians will be in the hearts of all men (Hebrews 8:8-11), and they will not misuse their democratic rights. Until then, sin will continue to lead men to vote for socialism, fascism, and communism.

The State as a Protector

All property is God's. He has established rules for the exchange, transmission, and development of this property. Theft is explicitly prohibited. God's law provides us with the case laws that enable us to define theft Biblically. For example, it is *not* theft if a traveller picks an apple from a tree and eats it as he goes along the road (Deuteronomy 23:24-25). Furthermore, it *is* theft if the owner of an agricultural property does not leave fallen fruit on the ground for gleaners (Deuteronomy 24:19). The Bible is our standard of what constitutes theft, not the British economist Adam Smith or Karl Marx.

The civil government is required by God to serve as the pro-

---

4. A. S. P. Woodhouse, *Puritanism and Liberty* (London: Dent, 1938), p. 53.
5. Karl Marx, "On the Jewish Question" (1843), in T. B. Bottomore (ed.), *Karl Marx: Early Writings* (New York: McGraw-Hill, 1964), pp. 11-12.

tector of property. It must honor the laws of ownership that are set forth in the Bible. It should not prosecute a man who takes a few ears of corn from his neighbor's field. Christ and the disciples were not guilty of theft when they did so (Matthew 12:1). The civil government can legitimately compel a farm owner to respect the gleaning laws. But the civil government cannot legitimately say which persons have to be allowed into the field to glean. The owner of the property has that responsibility, just as Boaz did (Ruth 2:3-12).

This view of theft and protection is not in conformity to either modern socialism or modern libertarianism. In the first system (socialism), the state collects the tithe for itself, and many times God's tithe, to be used for purposes specified by bureaucratic and political bodies. In the second system (libertarianism), all coercion against private property is defined as theft, including taxation itself (in some libertarian systems). Nevertheless, the Bible's standards are the valid ones, and the Bible is clear: *there is no absolute sovereignty in any person or institution*. Unquestionably, there are limits on the use of private property. But these limits are minimal. Given the Biblical standards of theft, the civil government becomes a legitimate sovereign in the area of theft prevention and punishment — not the only institution, but one of them, and the one that has the lawful authority to impose economic sanctions against thieves.

Economist R. H. Coase has stated emphatically: "A private-enterprise system cannot function properly unless property rights are created in resources, and, when this is done, someone wishing to use a resource has to pay the owner to obtain it."[6] The preservation of private ownership by the civil government against theft is, in and of itself, a foundation of Biblical capitalism. By *defining* the limits of ownership, and by *protecting* property from coercive attack from violent men and fraudulent practices, a godly civil government establishes the basis of economic growth and prosperity.

The words "mine" and "yours" are two of the most important

---

6. R. H. Coase, "The Federal Communications Commission," *Journal of Law and Economics*, II (1959), p. 14.

words in any society. Biblical preaching has, over centuries, enabled men to appreciate the importance of these two words. When the differences between the two are honored in law, word, and deed, society benefits. Men can better cooperate with each other in peaceful transactions precisely because of the *predictability* provided by a social order which recognizes "mine" and "yours." This facilitates the division of labor.

We need people to cooperate rather than wage war against each other. This requires that we allow other men to do what they want with whatever they own, so long as they do not violate God's civil laws. We must not forget the words of the owner of the vineyard in the parable of the vineyard:

> Is it not lawful for me to do what I want with my own things? Or is your eye evil because I am good? (Matthew 20:15).

Economist Harold Demsetz has seen the importance of property rights from the perspective of *social cooperation.*

> Property rights are an instrument of society and derive their significance from the fact that they help a man form those expectations which he can reasonably hold in his dealings with others. These expectations find expression in the laws, customs, and mores of a society. An owner of property rights possesses the consent of fellow men to allow him to act in particular ways.[7]

Men can make contracts with each other, and enjoy the fruits of their decisions concerning the stewardship of God's resources. To return to a now-familiar theme, *property rights reduce the zones of uncertainty in life.*

The State as Savior

The state is a messianic institution in the modern world, and it is a destroyer of capital. The Moloch state consumes the economic future of its worshippers, and the economic future of its

---

7. Demsetz, "Toward a Theory of Property Rights" (1967), in E. G. Furubotn and S. Pejovich (eds.), *The Economics of Property Rights* (Cambridge, Massachusetts: Ballinger, 1974), p. 31.

worshippers' heirs. The Moloch state, like the polluting factory, is a coercive, capital-destroying agent in the economy. But the polluting factory may provide productive employment for local residents, and it provides the consumers with lower-priced goods (lower priced than if the factory had to pay for pollution-control equipment). The state, in contrast, employs only bureaucrats, and uses its funds generally to subsidize the improvident members of society (some of whom may be quite rich), capturing them in a web of promised benefits, and destroying their incentive to work for the benefit of consumers.

But how can rich people be improvident? By "improvident," I mean "one who wastes his capital, or the capital entrusted to him by others." This certainly applies to senior executives of major industrial companies that apply to the Federal government for financial aid, tariffs, and other stolen economic goods.

The very poor also suffer a reduction of their opportunities to obtain the work skills they need to advance themselves in modern economic society. The confiscatory state is a far greater threat to property and freedom than some local factory which pollutes the air or water.

The modern state is a threat to human rights, for it is a threat to property rights. The modern state is a destroyer of human rights, for it is a destroyer of property rights. Guilt-ridden intellectuals, politicians, and sons of the rich have promoted an ideology of wealth-redistribution that destroys capital, and therefore destroys human aspirations. They have used the misleading slogan, "human rights above property rights," to destroy both human rights and property rights. They have adopted as their commandment, "Thou shalt not steal, except by majority vote." The result, increasingly, is the *decapitalization* of the formerly Christian West.

Never forget: a state that claims to be a savior of mankind necessarily becomes the final judge of mankind.

Summary

The Biblical doctrine of ownership is a doctrine of stewardship. God's property is to be carefully developed by His servants. The servants have chosen to ignore God, and they have also chosen to ignore His commandment against theft. Modern man has adopted a new theology, the ownership of property by the state. The state, as the sovereign owner, delegates to its servants the right to administer its property, but the state then insists on its share, its tithe. The tithe principle is built into the creation; the only question is this: *Who gets the tithe?* The state is collecting its tithe. As one economist has summarized it: "Win, and the state wins with you; lose, and you lose alone." That is the rule for the rich and the middle class, in any case.

The modern state is a thief. When Samuel warned the nation of Israel against selecting a king to rule over them, he tried to scare them by telling them that the king would extract a tithe of 10% (1 Samuel 8:15-17). The greatest bureaucratic dynasty of the ancient world, Egypt, took 20% as its tithe (Genesis 47:26). There is not a Western industrial state that extracts as little as Egypt took. In fact, in most instances, a tax rate of one-fifth of a nation's productivity would constitute a tax *reduction* of at least 50%.

Private property reduces uncertainty. It gives men an incentive to produce. It expands men's time horizons to unborn generations. It encourages economic growth by enabling innovators and workers to capture the value of their increased productivity. It encourages thrift. Being familistic in nature, it promotes the central institution of dominion. It allows the transfer of information, the transfer of risk, and the transfer of capital to those who are willing and able to bear the economic responsibilities of ownership. The protection of private property is one of the cornerstones of civilization. The civil government is to protect private property, not steal it.

The rise of the messianic state has threatened civilization. It is the greatest single danger today to the preservation and expansion of familistic capital. The envy-dominated ideologies of wealth-distribution through coercion—Marxism, socialism, Keynesianism, and the "social gospel"—have captured the minds of the intellectuals and political leaders. Unless this process is reversed, these anti-Biblical doctrines will decapitalize the modern world.

In summary:

1. The economy is not a covenant institution: no self-maledictory oath.

2. Marxist liberation theologians have made an attack on the free market central to their case.

3. The eighth commandment prohibits theft.

4. Private property rights (rights of *people* to own property) are basic to dominion.

5. Christian economics begins with this presupposition: God owns the world.

6. All human ownership is stewardship before God and other men.

7. Economic institutions are hierarchical.

8. The equality of wealth is a satanic goal.

9. The Bible teaches that there is a close relationship between poverty and laziness.

10. Long-term poverty is a specific curse of God on a rebellious society.

11. Wealth flows to those who work hard and honestly.

12. The free market provides the greatest upward social and economic mobility.

13. The politics of the welfare state teaches class conflict.

14. It is immoral to teach people that freedom is rigged against honesty and hard work.

15. Socialism is a conscious philosophy of destruction.

16. When propertyless people can vote away other men's property, society has in principle become socialist (Karl Marx).

17. The civil government is supposed to be a protector, including a protector of people's property.

18. This involves defining property rights.

19. The goal is social cooperation.

20. The modern humanist state seeks to become mankind's savior (and final judge).

21. Modern socialism threatens to decapitalize the world.

10

THE INEVITABILITY OF LIBERATION

And you shall remember the LORD your God: for it is He who
gives you power to get wealth, that He may establish His covenant
which He swore to your fathers, as it is this day (Deuteronomy 8:18).

This verse is crucial to understanding the relationship between
Biblical law and Christian progress over time. God grants gifts to
covenantally faithful societies. These gifts are given by God in
order to reinforce men's confidence in the trustworthiness of His
covenant, and so lead them to even greater faithfulness, which in
turn leads to additional blessings. Visible blessings are to serve as
confirmations of the covenant. God therefore gives men health and
wealth "that He may establish His covenant." When men respond
in faith and obedience, a system of *visible positive feedback* is created.

Biblical history is linear. It has a beginning (creation), meaning (sin and redemption), and an end (final judgment). It was
Augustine's emphasis on linear history over pagan cyclical history
that transformed the historical thinking of the West.[1] But the Biblical view of history is more than linear. It is *progressive*. It involves
visible cultural expansion. It is this faith in cultural progress
which has been unique to modern Western civilization. This optimistic outlook was secularized by seventeenth-century Enlight-
enment thinkers,[2] and by the Communists,[3] and its waning in the

---

1. Charles Norris Cochrane, *Christianity and Classical Culture: A Study in Thought
and Action from Augustus to Augustine* (New York: Oxford University Press, [1944]
1957), pp. 480-83.
2. Robert A. Nisbet, "The Year 2000 and All That," *Commentary* (June 1968).
3. F. N. Lee, *Communist Eschatology* (Nutley, New Jersey: Craig Press, 1974).

twentieth century threatens the survival of Western humanistic civilization.[4]

Dominion Theology vs. Pessimism

Victory in history is an inescapable concept. There can be no question of victory, either of covenant-keepers or covenant-breakers. The only question is: *Who will win?* If covenant-breakers rebel against Biblical law, and they become externally consistent with their own anti-God and anti-Biblical law presuppositions, then they will become historically impotent.

There is no neutrality anywhere in the universe. But since there is no intellectual and moral neutrality, then there can be no cultural, civic, or any other kind of public institutional neutrality. So which kind of worldview produces productive people? The liberation offered by Jesus Christ or the liberation offered by Karl Marx? Which offers positive blessings from the hand of God? Which will produce judgment from God?

Some Christians argue that it is the reprobate who will be nearly victorious in history, not Christians. Only at the end of time do the covenant-breakers have to face the fact of their defeat, when God brings His final judgment.

Consider what this means. It means that Christianity does not work. Here is what the pessimists are saying:

> "As Christians work out their own salvation with fear and trembling (Philippians 2:12), improving their creeds, improving their cooperation with each other on the basis of agreement about the creeds, as they learn about the law of God as it applies in their own era, as they become skilled in applying the law of God that they have learned about, they become culturally impotent. They become infertile, also, it would seem. They do not become fruitful and multiply. Or if they do their best to follow this commandment, they are left without the blessing of God—a blessing which He has promised to those who follow the laws He has established. In short,

---

4. Robert Nisbet, *History of the Idea of Progress* (New York: Basic Books, 1980), ch. 9 and Epilogue.

the increase of philosophical and moral self-awareness on the part of Christians leads to cultural impotence.

"On the other hand, as rebels develop their philosophy of anti-nomianism—the religion of evolutionary chaos or the religion of revolution—they become more powerful. As they depart from the presuppositions concerning God, man, law, and time that made possible Western technology and economic growth, they become richer. As they learn who they are and who God is, they appropriate the fruits of the righteous."

In short, except at the day of judgment, the following Bible verse is *not* true: "A good man leaves an inheritance to his children's children: and the wealth of the sinner is stored up for the righteous" (Proverbs 13:22).

Yes, every Christian admits that after the day of judgment, resurrected Christians inherit everything. But after the resurrection, the world will be transformed. If the church loses in its historical task, then it will not have even the memory of how God blesses covenantal faithfulness with external victory. There will be no physical inheritance of the victorious humanists' wealth. What good would it do sin-free resurrected Christians to inherit the filthy cultural rags of the pre-resurrection world? What good would it do to have God hand back to immortal, sin-free people the accumulated wealth of anti-God, self-consistent humanists? And why would these humanists have been able to operate God's pre-resurrection world in the first place? Our world operates in terms of law, meaning God's covenantal law, but consistent sinners would obviously refuse to abide by such covenantal laws, *assuming* that they were acting consistently with their religious presuppositions.

We need to discuss the foundation of victory in history as the Bible presents it. I tie my discussion of the principles of victory to the covenant structure of Deuteronomy. *The tool of dominion that God gives to His people is His revealed law.* Abandon Biblical law, and you thereby abandon any hope of long-term victory. Abandon your commitment to Biblical law, and you become an antinomian.

Those who predict the failure of the mission of the church in worldwide evangelism are saying that Satan will win in history's struggles until that final day that ends history (Revelation 20). The church fails in its mission to evangelize the world, disciple the nations, and subdue the earth to the glory of God. This is the heart and soul of the pessimist's theory of history. *The church fails.* He may talk victory—indeed, the language of pessimists is filled with victorious-sounding phrases—but he really means historical defeat.

Christians are humble before God, but confident before the creation which they are called by God to subdue. After all, they have Biblical law and the Holy Spirit. This confidence eventually leads the Christians into historic defeat and disaster, say the pessimists. But why should Christians lose? Why should obedience to God's laws produce failure? Why should the gospel message fail, when it produces good fruit?

Ethical rebels are arrogant before God, and claim that all nature is ruled by the meaningless laws of probability—ultimate chaos, including moral chaos. Those who predict the failure of the church say of the humanists and Communists that by immersing themselves in the philosophy of moral and revolutionary chaos— the religion of revolution—covenant-breakers will somehow be able to emerge totally victorious across the whole face of the earth, a victory which is called to a halt only by the physical intervention of Jesus Christ at the final judgment. A commitment to lawlessness leads to external victory. This makes no sense theologically, let alone morally.

Evil's Lever: Good

Covenant-breakers must do good externally in order to increase their ability to do evil. They need to use the lever of God's law in order to increase their influence. These rebels will not be able to act consistently with their own religious and intellectual presuppositions and still be able to exercise power. They want power more than they want philosophical consistency. This is especially true of Western covenant-breakers who live in the shadow of Christian dominion theology. In short, *they restrain the working out of the implications of their own consistency.* Believers in randomness, chaos, and meaningless, the power-seekers nevertheless choose structure, discipline, and the rhetoric of ultimate victory.

If a modern investigator would like to see as fully consistent a pagan culture as one might imagine, he could visit the African tribe, the Ik ("eek"). Colin Turnbull did, and his book, *The Mountain People* (1973), is a classic. He found almost total rebellion against law — family law, civic law, all law. Yet he also found a totally impotent, beaten tribal people who were rapidly becoming extinct. They were harmless to the West because they were more self-consistent that the West's Satanists.

The difference between the humanist power-seekers and the more fully consistent but suicidal tribal pagans is the difference between the Communists and the Ik. It is the difference between power religion and escape religion. Some Eastern mystic who seeks escape through ascetic techniques of withdrawal, or some Western imitator with an alpha-wave machine and earphones ("Become an instant electronic yogi!"), is acting far more consistently with the anti-Christian philosophy of ultimate meaninglessness than a Communist revolutionary is. The yogi is not fully consistent: he still needs discipline techniques, and discipline implies an orderly universe. But he is more consistent than the Communist. He is not seeking the salvation of a world of complete illusion (maya) through the exercise of power.

Satan's Inconsistency

Satan needs a chain of command in order to exercise power. Thus, in order to create the greatest havoc for the church, Satan and his followers need to imitate the church. Like the child who needs to sit on his father's lap in order to slap him, so does the God-hating rebel need a crude imitation of God's dominion theology in order to exercise power. A child who rejects the idea of his father's lap cannot seriously hope to slap him. The anti-Christian has officially adopted an "anti-lap" theory of existence. He admits no cause-and-effect relationship between lap and slap. To the extent that he acts consistently with this view, he becomes impotent to attack God's people.

This means that with an increase in consistent living, the *ethical* aspects of the separation between the saved and the lost become more and more fundamental. Unbelievers recognize more and more how much they hate God and how different they are from Christians, but the increasing self-understanding on the part of the power-seeking unbeliever does not lead him to *apply* Satan's philosophy of ultimate meaninglessness and chaos; it leads him instead to apply Satan's counterfeit of dominion religion, the religion of power.

The unbeliever can achieve power only by refusing to become fully consistent with Satan's religion of chaos. He needs organization and capital — God's gifts of life, knowledge, law, and time — in order to produce maximum destruction. Like the Soviet Union, which has always had to import or steal the bulk of its technology from the West in order to build up an arsenal to destroy the West,[5] so does the Satanist have to import Christian intellectual and moral capital in order to wage an effective campaign against the church.

First, the Christian exercises dominion by becoming more consistent with the Christian faith that he holds, meaning morally and logically consistent with the new man within him, and therefore by adhering ever more closely to God's law. Biblical law is the covenant-keeper's *fully self-consistent tool of dominion.*

Second, the covenant-breaker exercises power by becoming *inconsistent* with his ultimate philosophy of randomness. He can commit effective crimes only by *stealing the worldview of Christians.* The bigger the crimes he wishes to commit (the ethical impulse of evil), the more carefully he must plan (the moral impulse of righteousness: counting the costs [Luke 14:28-30]). The Christian can work to fulfill the dominion covenant through a life of consistent

---

5. Antony Sutton, *The Best Enemy Money Can Buy* (Billings, Montana: Liberty House, 1986). On the technological dependence of the Soviet Union on commercial Western imports, see also Sutton, *Western Technology and Soviet Economic Development*, 3 Volumes (Stanford, California: Hoover Institution Press, 1968-73); Charles Levinson, *Vodka Cola* (London: Gordon & Cremonesi, 1978); Joseph Finder, *Red Carpet* (New York: Holt, Rinehart & Winston, 1983).

thought and action; the anti-Christian can achieve an offensive, destructive campaign against the Christians — as contrasted with a consistently satanic self-destructive life of drugs and debauchery — only by stealing the Biblical worldview and twisting it to evil purposes.

In short, *to become really evil you need to become pretty good.*

The Bible says that all those who hate God love death (Proverbs 8:36b). Therefore, for God-haters to live consistently, they would have to commit suicide. It is not surprising that the French existentialist philosopher Albert Camus was fascinated with the possibility of suicide. It was consistent with his philosophy of meaninglessness. To become a historic threat to Christians, unbelievers must *restrain their own ultimate impulse*, namely, the quest for death. Thus, their increase in self-consistency over time is incomplete, until the final rebellion, when their very act of rebellion brings on the final judgment.

This will be the final culmination in history of Satan's earlier act of envious defiance in luring the mobs to crucify Christ: an act of violence that insured his total judgment and defeat. Yet he did it anyway, out of spite. When God finally removes His restraint on their suicidal impulse, they will launch their suicidal rebellion. The removal of God's restraint is always a prelude to judgment.

So the ethical war will escalate. Whom should we expect God to bless in this escalating ethical war? The Christian whose worldview is consistent and God-honoring, or the God-hater whose worldview is inconsistent and God-defying? Who will be burdened by greater moral and intellectual schizophrenia as time goes on and self-understanding increases? Whose plans of conquest will be inconsistent with his philosophy of existence, the Christian or the anti-Christian? Who is truly growing in self-understanding, the Christian or the anti-Christian?

The answers should be obvious. Unfortunately for Christian preaching in the twentieth century, pessimistic theologies make the obvious obscure, and they have been dominant since the 1930's.

Pessimism Has Things Backwards

It should be clear by now that the pessimistic Christians' version of the relationship between Biblical law and the creation is completely backwards. No doubt Satan wishes it were a true version. No doubt he wants his followers to believe that by progressively adhering to Biblical law, Christians will fall into increasing cultural impotence. No doubt he wants his followers to believe this preposterous error. But how can a consistent Christian believe it? How can a Christian believe that adherence to Biblical law produces cultural impotence, while commitment to philosophical chaos—the religion of satanic revolution—leads to cultural victory?

There is no doubt in my mind that the pessimists do not want to teach such a doctrine, yet that is where their pessimism inevitably leads. They refuse to acknowledge the future reality of Christian dominion on earth before the final judgment by means of the *positive feedback* aspect of covenantal blessings: from obedience to blessing to greater obedience.

Biblical law is basic to the fulfillment of the cultural mandate, also called the dominion covenant. It is our tool of dominion. There are only four possibilities concerning law: revealed law, natural law, chaos, or a syncretistic combination of the above (e.g., statistical regularity: a little natural law and a little randomness). Christian thinking in this century has outspokenly denied the first possibility: the binding character of Old Testament law in New Testament times. We do not find treatises on the contemporary application of Biblical law written by pessimistic Christian theologians.

When Christians once again begin to take God's revealed law seriously, no humanist movement will be able to roll back the expanding church. Christians will at last have put to use God's tool of dominion.

Empowering by the Spirit

The Christian needs to recognize that what distinguishes Biblical law in the New Testament era from the Old Covenant era is the vastly greater empowering of Christians by the Holy Spirit to obey the law.[6] The Spirit's empowering is a fundamental distinction between the two covenantal periods. But this greater empowering by the Spirit must be made manifest in history if it is to be distinguished from the repeated failure of believers in the Old Covenant era to stay in the "positive feedback" mode: blessings . . . greater faith . . . greater blessings, etc. It is this positive feedback aspect of Biblical law in New Testament times which links Biblical law with optimism toward the future (dominion theology).

Does the great power of the Holy Spirit really mean anything in history? If we were to argue that the greater empowering of the Holy Spirit in the New Testament era is only a kind of theoretical backdrop to history, and therefore Biblical law will not actually be preached and obeyed in this pre-final-judgment age, then we would really be abandoning the whole idea of the Holy Spirit's empowering of Christians and Christian society in history. Yet people argue this way: "Yes, the Spirit empowers Christians to obey Biblical law; however, they will not adopt or obey Biblical law in history."

Will the progressive manifestation of the fruits of obeying Biblical law also be strictly internal and not external? If so, then what has happened to the positive feedback aspect of covenant law? What has happened to empowering by the Holy Spirit?

I argue that the greater empowering by the Holy Spirit for God's people to obey and enforce Biblical law is what invalidates the implicit anti-dominion position regarding the ineffectiveness of Biblical law in New Testament times. If Christians obey God's law, then the positive feedback process is inevitable; it is part of the law-governed aspect of the creation: "from glory to glory" (2 Corinthians 3:18). If some segments of the church refuse to obey it, then those segments will eventually lose influence, money, and power. Their place will be taken by those Christian churches that obey God's laws, and that will therefore experience the covenant's

---

6. Greg L. Bahnsen, *By This Standard: The Authority of God's Law Today* (Tyler, Texas: Institute for Christian Economics, 1985), pp. 159-62, 185-86.

external blessings. These churches will spread the gospel more effectively as a result. This is the positive feedback aspect of Biblical law.

If we accept the possibility of a defense of God's law that rejects the historic inevitability of the long-term expansion of Christian dominion through the covenant's positive feedback, then we face a major problem: *how to explain the difference between the New Testament church and Old Testament Israel.* If the Christian church fails to build the visible kingdom by means of Biblical law and the power of the gospel, despite the resurrection of Christ and the presence of the Holy Spirit, then what kind of religion are we preaching? Why is the church a significant improvement culturally and socially over Old Testament Israel?

What does such a theology say about the gospel? What kind of power does the gospel offer men for the overcoming of the effects of sin in history? Is Satan's one-time success in tempting Adam never going to be overcome in history? Will Satan attempt to comfort himself throughout eternity with the thought that by defeating Adam, he made it impossible for mankind to work out the dominion covenant in history, even in the face of the death and resurrection of Christ? If we argue this way—the failure of a Spirit-empowered Biblical law-order to produce the visible kingdom—then we must find an answer to this question: Why is sin triumphant in history, in the face of the gospel?

Then there is the impolite but inevitable question: *Why is Jesus a loser in history?*

Pessimists, by preaching eschatological impotence culturally, thereby immerse themselves in quicksand—the quicksand of antinomianism. Some sands are quicker than others. Eventually, they swallow up anyone so foolish as to try to walk through them. Antinomianism leads into the pits of impotence and retreat. No one wants to risk everything he owns, including his life, in a battle his commander says will not be won. Only a few diehard souls will attempt it. You can build a ghetto with such a theology; you cannot build a civilization.

Biblical law must also be preached. It must be seen as the tool of cultural reconstruction. It must be seen as operating *now*, in New Testament times. It must be seen that there is a relationship between covenantal faithfulness and obedience to Biblical law — that without obedience there is no faithfulness, no matter how emotional believers may become, or how sweet the gospel tastes (for a while). Furthermore, there are external blessings that follow covenantal obedience to God's law-order.

How Can Christians Lose?

Christians overcome the world in the same way that they overcome sin in their own lives: by obeying God. We do not become less sinful by imitating the world of sin.

> And do not be conformed to this world, but be transformed by the renewing of your mind, that you may prove what is the good and acceptable and perfect will of God (Romans 12:2).

> Imitate me, even as I also imitate Christ (1 Corinthians 11:1).

Neither do we become more powerful by imitating the humanist's power religion. The Christian is called to *ethical self-consciousness*. Out of this comes increasing self-understanding. Ethics is the fundamental issue, not philosophical knowledge, and not political or military power.

The increase in the ethical understanding of Christians results in their increasing understanding of the Bible's principles of knowledge. Christians think God's thoughts after Him, as creatures made in His image.

> For though we walk in the flesh, we do not war according to the flesh. For the weapons of our warfare are not carnal, but mighty in God for pulling down strongholds, casting down arguments and every high thing that exalts itself against the knowledge of God, bringing every thought into captivity to the obedience of Christ (2 Corinthians 10:3-5).

The issue is *obedience*, not philosophical rigor. Obedience in the long run is what brings the church increasing wisdom and increasing philosophical rigor.

The follower of Satan cannot expect to match the church intellectually in the long run, for Christians have the mind of Christ ethically (1 Corinthians 2:16). The only thing that keeps covenant-breakers from going mad and committing suicide is that God restrains their ability to follow the logic of their anti-God presuppositions. God also restrains their suicidal impulses. He does this for the sake of His people, who in history need the cooperation and added productivity of the unregenerate. God restrains them simply to make them productive. Without God's restraint, they would be powerless.

This is why *the kingdom of God will win in any open competitive contest with Satan's rival kingdoms*. Christians unfortunately do not believe this in our era, which is why they are so fearful. They see the satanic world system getting worse, evil getting richer, and Christian influence declining. The kingdom of righteousness in their view cannot survive a fair fight, let alone an unfair fight. They conclude that God's people are doomed to be historical losers.

Abandoning Responsibility

They simultaneously believe that since Christians cannot win in open competition — socially, intellectually, culturally, economically — any attempt to establish Biblical law as the foundation of law and order must be the recommendation of potential tyrants. "After all, if these people are really trying to build a self-consciously Christian society, and if they really expect to win, then they must be planning to impose tyrannical force. We know that Christianity cannot defeat the power religion. Therefore, any program that proposes such a victory must have as its hidden agenda a rival program of power."

Christians have generally accepted as valid the worldview of the power religion. They have concluded that power, and only power, is the basis of successful political programs. They have accepted Mao's dictum that power (and everything else) grows out of the barrel of a gun. They do not accept the operating principle of the dominion religion, namely, that long-term authority is the product of a bottom-up extension of God's strategy of dominion, beginning with self-government under Biblical law. They do not believe that Biblical law produces social peace and prosperity. Thus, fearing the responsibilities of dominion because they mistake dominion for tyrannical power, and because they do not want to be labeled *Christian* tyrants, Christians: (1) seek to become powerful themselves in terms of humanism's acceptable political strategies; (2) seek an alliance with humanistic power religionists against the dominion religion; or (3) retreat from the public arena in an attempt to escape responsibility.

Christians generally do not believe that God in His providence designed the mind of man for the purpose of man's taking dominion. They do not believe that regenerate minds that necessarily possess the mind of Christ (1 Corinthians 2:16) are dominically superior to unregenerate minds that have the mind of Satan. Thus, Christians have retreated time and again in the cultural and intellectual battles. They have justified these repeated retreats by devising eschatologies of inevitable, guaranteed defeat for the visible kingdom of God. This makes it easier to run up the white flag. "What else could we expect but defeat? After all, we're Christians."

Our enemies have stolen the Bible's vision of victory and its doctrine of providence. They have reworked these doctrines to fit their requirements. *Christians are fearful of an enemy army that has stolen everything positive that it has in its arsenal.* Christians do not see that it is our God who makes the rules. In contrast, our enemy knows what wins. Satan cannot win if his followers cling to his own doctrine of chaos. This is why he has stolen our vision and worldview.

Who has the right to adopt such a program of victory? Whose Commander gave a death blow to His rival's head (Genesis 3:15) at Calvary? Admittedly, the church suffers from a limp, just as Jacob did (Genesis 32:25). The church's heel is injured, just as God promised that Christ's would be (Genesis 3.15). But the enemy's head is crushed. When going into battle, which wound would you prefer to march with? A crushed head or an injured heel?

Unbelievers appear to be culturally dominant today. Chris-

tians have for too long seen themselves as the dogs sitting beneath
the humanists' tables, hoping for an occasional scrap of unenriched
white bread to fall their way. They worry about their own competence. They think of themselves as second-class citizens. And
the humanists, having spotted this self-imposed "second-class citizen" mentality, have taken advantage of it.

The Five Doctrines for Dominion on Earth

Believers have for over a century retreated into antinomian
pietism and pessimism. This retreat began in the 1870's. They
have lost the vision of victory which once motivated Christians to
evangelize and then take over the Roman Empire. They have
abandoned faith in one or more of the five features of Christian
social philosophy that make progress possible: (1) the absolute
sovereignty of the Creator God; (2) God's covenant that governs
all men; (3) the tool of the covenant, *Biblical law*; (4) Biblical presuppositionalism—the self-attesting truth of an infallible Bible,
which is the ultimate judge of everything; and (5) the dynamic of
eschatological optimism. We should conclude, then, that either the
dissolution of modern humanist culture is at hand, or else the regenerate must regain sight of their lost theological heritage: dominion optimism and Biblical law.

The Communists have a perverted version of all five points.
This is why they are such powerful rivals to Christians. *First*, they
believe in the sovereignty of man, as manifested in our day by the
Communist Party, the "vanguard of the proletariat," which is infallible. *Second*, they believe in a covenant: membership in the
Communist Party, which is rigorously hierarchical. *Third*, they believe that socialist law, socialist institutions, and socialist everything are the product of a unique philosophy. They believe in
their exclusive way of accomplishing things. *Fourth*, they believe
in the providence of the impersonal forces of dialectical history,
which their leaders alone understand perfectly in any historical
period. The Party executes infallible judgments because it has access to their "holy writ": Marxism-Leninism. They do not appeal
to any other logic, any other source of authority except their own

"infallible" books. They have complete confidence in Marxism-Leninism. *Fifth*, they are optimists (outside the Soviet Union, anyway). They believe that the forces of history have guaranteed their historic victory. They look for the inevitable victory of Marxism in the future. They believe in the power of revolutionary violence to transform this world.

We see a similar confidence in radical Islam, another powerful historic rival to Christianity. *First*, Muslims believe in a sovereign God, Allah. Allah predestines everything. This faith is sometimes fatalistic, but it leads to long-term confidence. *Second*, they believe in a covenantal religious organization that is closely allied to a military hierarchy. They are called to triumph over their foes in battle. *Third*, they believe in Islamic law and Islamic civilization. They believe that the West offers them nothing. They believe that their way is the only valid way. *Fourth*, they believe in their "holy writ," the Koran. They appeal to no other writings or logic to prove the truth of the Koran. They have complete confidence in it. *Fifth*, they do not think they can lose. Allah has willed their victory.

Modern humanistic science has been another major religious rival to Christianity. Until quite recently, science has held all five points. *First*, for the providence of God, scientists substituted the rule of inescapable cause and effect. Their universe seemed to be governed by strict causality that the scientific method can master, thereby transferring power over nature (and other men) to the scientific elite. *Second*, this elite maintains discipline through granting access to teaching positions, scholarly publishing, and government research grants. From full professor to associate professor, to assistant professor, to instructor: hierarchy prevails. *Third*, it has had confidence in the scientific tool of dominion, scientific method: experiments and mathematics. The rise of the computer seemed to offer even more reason to believe in this methodological tool. *Fourth*, they have believed in presuppositionalism: the self-attesting truth of a nearly infallible method—not infallible, but more perfect than any rival group possesses. Science has been regarded as a self-attesting truth, a truth which validates all other forms of this-worldly knowledge, especially religion. Scientific method judges all rival forms of this-worldly truth. *Fifth*, scientists have been highly optimistic about the potential for bettering men's lives through science and technology. Science will free mankind from the limits of scarcity and ignorance! This faith in science was especially strong prior to World War I.

In short, these five points are basic to a vision of victory. They have motivated the most powerful, world-transforming movements in man's history. But now that the faith of Christianity's rivals is waning, Christians have a unique historical opportunity to recapture the minds of men with the Bible's vision of victory. But this requires that Christians become confident in Christianity. This means that they must also have confidence in the earthly future, for *a religion whose principles do not guarantee earthly success for its followers as a covenanted community is not a religion which inspires confidence.*

Restoration

Christians must call the external culture's guidelines back to God's revealed law. They must regain the leadership they forfeited when they adopted as Christian the speculations of self-proclaimed "reasonable" apostates. If this is not done, then we will slide back once more, until the unbelievers at last resemble that African tribe, the Ik, and the Christians can begin the process of cultural domination once more. If neither happens, then society will return eventually to barbarism.

Understandably, I pray for the regeneration of the ungodly *and* the rediscovery of Biblical law and accurate Biblical eschatology on the part of present Christians and future converts. Whether we will see such a revival in our day is unknown to me. There are reasons to believe that it can and will happen.[7] There are also reasons to doubt such optimism. The Lord knows.

---

7. Gary North, *The Sinai Strategy: Economics and the Ten Commandments* (Tyler, Texas: Institute for Christian Economics, 1986), pp. 86-92: "The Sabbath Millennium."

We must abandon antinomianism and pessimistic eschatologies that are inherently antinomian. We must call men back to faith in the God of the whole Bible. We must affirm that in the plan of God there will come a day of increased self-awareness, when men will call churls churlish and liberal men gracious (Isaiah 32). This will be a day of great external blessings—the greatest in history. Long ages of such self-awareness unfold before us. And at the end of time comes a generation of rebels who know churls from liberals, and who then wage war against the godly (Revelation 20:7-8). They will lose this final campaign of evil (Revelation 20:9).[8]

Why should Christians remain pessimistic about their earthly future? Will God destroy His *preliminary down payment* (preliminary manifestation) of the New Heavens and the New Earth (Isaiah 65:17-20)? Will God erase the sign that His Word has been obeyed in history, that the dominion covenant has been nearly fulfilled by regenerate people? Will Satan, that great destroyer, have the joy of seeing God's Word thwarted, His church's handiwork torn down by Satan's very hordes? The pessimist answers yes. The dominion optimist must deny it with all his strength.

There is continuity in life, despite discontinuities. The wealth of the sinner is laid up for the just. Satan would like to burn God's field, but he cannot. The tares and wheat grow to maturity, and then the reapers go out to harvest the wheat, cutting away the chaff and tossing it into the fire (Matthew 13:24-43).

Satan would like to turn back the final judgment of God on sin, return to ground zero, return to the garden of Eden, when the dominion covenant was first given. He cannot do this. History moves forward toward the fulfillment of the dominion covenant— as much a fulfillment as pre-final-judgment mankind can achieve. At that point, Satan will use the last of his time and the last of his power to strike out against God's people. When he uses his gifts to become finally, totally destructive, he is cut down from above.

---

8. Gary North, *Dominion and Common Grace: The Biblical Basis of Progress* (Tyler, Texas: Institute for Christian Economics, 1987).

And the meek — meek before God, and therefore active toward His creation — shall at last inherit the earth. A renewed earth and renewed heaven is the final payment by God the Father to His Son and to those He has given to His Son. But prior to this, Christianity will reign victorious on earth. This is dominion theology's expectation.

Summary

Those who are ethically subordinate to Satan can nevertheless receive external blessings if they obey God's law externally. At the final day, they will rebel. Thus, the believer in dominion theology does not preach that the whole world will someday be populated exclusively by regenerate people.

By denying the legitimacy of Old Testament law in New Testament times, Christians thereby abandon the tool of dominion which God has given to His people to fulfill the terms of the dominion covenant ("cultural mandate"). They have abandoned God's program of "positive feedback" — the progressive sanctification of civilization. They have therefore abandoned the Bible's eschatology of *victory in history.*

If the conditional promises of Deuteronomy 28:1-14 are taken seriously, and our empowering by the Holy Spirit is taken seriously, then the doctrine of historical progress can be taken seriously. This progress must become externalized through the Biblical system of positive feedback (Deuteronomy 8:18). To deny such historical, institutional progress, the pessimist must reject Biblical law.

A war is in progress — a war with humanism. Humanism will not respect Christian sanctuaries. Humanism must be defeated. Biblical law is the weapon, with Christians empowered by the Holy Spirit. Christians who believe in dominion theology call men to pick up God's weapon, Biblical law, to carry with them when they bring the gospel to the lost. There can be no more excuses for cultural impotence.

Christians have the tool of dominion. It will do no good to say that Christians cannot win in history, for we have the weapons to win. Any excuse now is simply an unwillingness to join the battle. But as in the days of Deborah, there are many who choose not to fight. And some day, some future Deborah will sing a modern version of: "Gilead stayed beyond the Jordan, and why did Dan remain in ships? Asher continued at the seashore, and stayed by his inlets" (Judges 5:17).

If progress is seen as exclusively internal, or at most ecclesiastical, then history inescapably becomes antinomian. Biblical law must be abandoned. Problem: *Biblical law in New Testament times does not permit long-term failure.* Biblical law necessarily must lead to positive visible results, which in turn should reinforce faithfulness, as well as serve as a light to the unconverted (Deuteronomy 4:6-8), a city on a hill (Matthew 5:14).

In summary:

1. God grants external success to Christians who obey His law.

2. He does this to confirm their faith in the reliability of His covenant promises.

3. We can call this system of covenantal blessings *positive feedback*.

4. History is linear (straight line).

5. History is also progressive.

6. Victory is an inescapable concept.

7. The only question is: Who will win?

8. Some Christians preach the historical defeat of the church.

9. This means that there is no positive feedback aspect of God's law in history.

10. The Bible says that the wealth of the wicked is stored up for the righteous (Proverbs 13:22).

11. This makes no sense if this verse applies only to the sin-free world after the final judgment.

12. Biblical law is our tool of dominion.

13. Covenant-breakers must become inconsistent with Satan's philosophy and worldview if they are to gain power.

14. Christians can become more powerful by becoming more consistent with their God's worldview.

15. This is a major advantage Christians have over non-Christians: consistency works for Christians.

16. To gain much power, the Satanists must steal major sections of the Christians' worldview.

17. When Christians begin to take God's law seriously, they will begin to conquer the world.

18. The Holy Spirit has empowered Christians in a way that Old Testament believers were not empowered.

19. This empowering will become progressively manifest in history.

20. So why do some Christians believe that Jesus will be a loser in history?

21. Christians possess the five doctrines of earthly victory.

22. The major world-conquering rival religious movements have also held imitations of these five doctrines.

23. Their faith is waning.

24. Christians must work to restore men's faith in the validity of Biblical law.

25. Christians must abandon antinomianism and pessimism about the earthly future.

26. An era of great spiritual and economic blessings is ahead of us.

27. Satan will not thwart God's word and God's people in history.

28. Satan cannot turn back the clock, though he wants to.

29. The meek before God shall inherit the earth.

30. The positive feedback aspect of Biblical law does not permit external failure to Christians, who are empowered by the Holy Spirit to obey God.

CONCLUSION

All things have been delivered to Me by the Father, and no one knows the Son except through the Father. Nor does anyone know the Father except through the Son, and he to whom the Son wills to reveal Him. Come to Me, all you who labor and are heavy laden, and I will give you rest. Take My yoke upon you and learn from Me, for I am gentle and lowly in heart, and you will find rest for your souls. For My yoke is easy and My burden light (Matthew 11:29-30).

There is only one way to find true liberation: to be in *subjection to Jesus Christ*. There is only one alternative to being in subjection to Jesus Christ: being in subjection to Satan. Therefore, there is only one alternative to liberation: slavery.

We are always under the domination of someone who is more powerful than we are. We live under hierarchy. We are either under Christ or under Satan. There is no autonomy for man. There is no self-law. We do not build civilizations all by ourselves. We are either under Christ or under Satan. We work to build a Christian civilization or a satanic civilization; we cannot legitimately hope to build man's autonomous civilization. No such civilization is possible.

If we as individuals can find true liberty only under Jesus Christ, then why should we expect to find a society that provides true liberty that is not under Jesus Christ? If true freedom is only available to us as *individuals* under God and God's law, then why should we expect to find civil liberty under Satan and Satan's law (which is in fact lawlessness)? There is no "natural liberty" under "natural law" enforced by "natural man."

But the natural man does not receive the things of the Spirit of God, for they are foolishness to him; nor can he know them, because they are spiritually discerned. But he who is spiritual judges all things, yet he himself is rightly judged by no one. For "who has known the mind of the Lord that he might instruct Him?" (Isaiah 40:13).

But we have the mind of Christ (1 Corinthians 2:14-16).

There is true liberty only under Jesus Christ. Until Christians really believe this, and preach it against all false philosophies of humanism, they will not find freedom.

Under Christ

What does it mean to be under Jesus Christ? It means being under His law.

If you love Me, keep My commandments (John 14:15).

Now by this we know that we know Him, if we keep His commandments. He who says, "I know Him," and does not keep His commandments, is a liar, and the truth is not in him. But whoever keeps His word, truly the love of God is perfected in him. By this we know that we are in Him. He who says he abides in Him ought himself to walk just as He walked. Brethren, I write no new commandment to you, but an old commandment which you have had from the beginning. The old commandment is the word which you heard from the beginning (1 John 2:3-7).

But he who looks into the perfect law of liberty and continues in it, and is not a forgetful hearer but a doer of the work, this one will be blessed in what he does (James 1:25).

And take not the word of truth utterly out of my mouth, for I have hoped in Your ordinances. So shall I keep Your law continually, forever and ever. And I will walk at liberty, for I seek your precepts. I will speak of Your testimonies also before kings, and will not be ashamed (Psalm 119:43-46).

Liberty and God's law: the two are inseparable. He who preaches against the law of God preaches against liberty. Anyone who says that we can build our lives, our families, our churches, or our civil governments on any foundation other than the law of God, and still have liberty, is a liar. He is a deceiver. He is laying the foundation of tyranny.

This means that a person who speaks in the name of Jesus Christ must speak the *whole* counsel of God. He must preach the *whole* law of God. He must not limit himself to a chapter or two in Exodus, the Book of Amos, Acts 2 and 4, and 2 Corinthians 8. No, he must preach the whole law. He must not preach selectively, building a case for armed revolution on the basis of one or two Scriptures, while ignoring everything the Bible says about private property, hard work, faithfulness to wives and children, obedience to superiors, and the God-given right for a property-owner to do what he wants with what he owns.

> Is it now lawful for me to do what I wish with my own things? Or is your eye evil because I am good? (Matthew 20:15).

There are many preachers who come in the name of Christ whose eye is evil. Some of them even have two eyes that are evil. They preach liberation through theft. They preach peace through terrorism. They preach prosperity through bureaucracy. They preach liberation through civil government. They preach salvation by legislation. The liberation they preach is the march into slavery. They preach compassion through class conflict. They preach justice through revolution. They preach Jesus through the eyes of Karl Marx, a dedicated atheist. They preach lies in the name of the gospel.

What does the gospel teach? It teaches contentment with one's condition, but it also teaches about prayer, hard work, faithfulness to one's wife, and the hope of eventual liberation *in history*. The gospel says that liberty is better than slavery, but if slavery is for a while our assigned condition, then to make the best of it. Paul writes:

> Let each one remain in the same calling in which he was called. Were you called while a slave? Do not be concerned about it; but if you can be made free, rather use it. For he who is called in the Lord while a slave is the Lord's freedman. Likewise he who is

called while free is Christ's slave. You were bought with a price; do not become slaves of men. Brethren, let each one remain with God in that calling in which he was called (1 Corinthians 7:20-24).

If we were converted to Christ as men under another man's jurisdiction, let us remain faithful slaves until the day that God brings us an opportunity for freedom. The Hebrews in captivity had to serve as slaves and unfree men for a time, but God eventually heard their groaning and their prayers. He delivered them out of bondage to men and false gods *so that they could obey Him better as free men.* We are called to freedom *in order to obey God better.* So, if we are not living today in the freedom that the gospel offers, *let us do our best today as unfree men to obey God as best we can.* This will train us to be better servants of God — and better free men — when He delivers us.

We are not to choose slavery. Slavery to Marxism is the worst kind of slavery. Paul warned us, "You were bought with a price; do not *become* slaves of men." God warned Isaac:

> "Do not go down to Egypt; dwell in the land of which I shall tell you. Sojourn in this land, and I will be with you and bless you; for to you and your descendants I give all these lands, and I will perform the oath which I swore to Abraham your father. And I will make your descendants multiply as the stars of heaven; I will give to your descendants all these lands; and in your seed all the nations of the earth shall be blessed" (Genesis 26:2-4).

Do not go down to Egypt, no matter how hard it seems to you in the wilderness. In Egypt there is slavery, no matter how great the promises seem, no matter how fine the land of Goshen looks. Stay out of Egypt! In our day, the land of Marxism is the land of Egypt.

What would Isaac receive? Not the promised land. God promised to bless his descendants, but He made no special promise to Isaac. Isaac was to remain content, despite the fact that he would not personally inherit the land in his lifetime. He had the promise of God: *his descendants would inherit the land.* That was to be sufficient for Isaac.

And why would this promise come true? Because of faithfulness—God's and Abraham's. Abraham had been faithful:

". . . because Abraham obeyed My voice and kept My charge, My commandments, My statutes, and My laws" (Genesis 26:5).

Did Isaac obey? Yes. "So Isaac dwelt in Gerar" (Genesis 26:6). Gerar was not the final goal; the promised land was. But Isaac was to be content in Gerar for the time being, until God moved him somewhere else.

We, too, are to remain in Gerar.

We are not to ignore the present evil around us. We are not to pretend that evil does not exist. We are certainly not to teach that evil is good, or that oppression is compassion. We are to work and pray for a better day *on earth* when all men will recognize evil for what it is. We are to work and pray for the day promised by Isaiah:

The foolish person will no longer be called generous, nor the miser said to be bountiful. For the foolish person will speak foolishness, and his heart will work iniquity: to practice ungodliness, to utter error against the LORD, to keep the hungry unsatisfied, and he will cause the drink of the thirsty to fail. Also the schemes of the schemer are evil; he devises wicked plans to destroy the poor with lying words, even when the needy speaks justice. But a generous man devises generous things, and by generosity he shall stand (Isaiah 32:5-8).

Not by revolution shall the generous person stand, but by generosity. A better world *on earth* is coming:

Then justice will dwell in the wilderness, and righteousness remain in the fruitful field. The work of righteousness will be peace, and the effect of righteousness, quietness and assurance forever. My people will dwell in a peaceful habitation, in secure dwellings, and in quiet resting places (Isaiah 32:16-18).

Faithful Christians are not to preach perpetual contentment with moral evil, either personal or social, but neither are we to preach instant liberation through revolution and violence. Christians are to preach life, not death. We are to be content with life as

God has given it to us, which includes the gift of time and the obligation to preach the gospel. We are to work to overcome evil, first through *self*-government under God's law. We are to do what Joseph did in the Egyptian prison: ask the butler (cup-bearer) to remember us when he gets back in the house of the king (Genesis 40:14), but when he forgets (40:23), we are still to be the best, most reliable people in the prison, until such time as God frees us. This is how we get the prison-keeper to delegate more responsibility to us (Genesis 39:22-23). The more responsibility we receive, the more opportunities we have to prove ourselves before God as His faithful, obedient servants. After all, this is what God wants: *faithful servants*. This is why He grants us more freedom. He is not interested in granting us more freedom so that we can become *unfaithful* servants.

Self-Government Under God's Law

Liberation is a legitimate goal, both personally and corporately: *liberation from sin* for the individual, the family, the church, and the civil government. There is only one theology that can produce liberation: Biblical Christianity. It teaches a very different outlook from that taught by "liberation theology." The theology known today as liberation theology is simply an apology for bureaucratic socialism, Marxism, and political theft on an international scale. Liberation theology is simply Marxism dressed in clerical robes. It is a gospel of "salvation through political plunder."

The Bible teaches a system of personal freedom and personal responsibility under God. It teaches *self-government under God's law*. Remove the continuing validity of God's revealed law from your theology, and you thereby remove the Biblical basis of self-government. Antinomianism produces impotence and slavery. It leads to relativism. It also produces legalism as a reaction against relativism: man's authoritative laws rather than God's.

The Bible also teaches covenant theology. The covenants of God are marked by a five-point structure that offers men release from tyranny. When God's covenant structure is respected in society's institutions, it becomes possible for people to work out their salvation with fear and trembling without having to ask for permission from men.

The Bible teaches decentralization, the division of labor, and the specialization of production (1 Corinthians 12). This decentralized social order is ideal for allowing people with new insights and innovations to prove the worth of their ideas to their fellow men. It produces responsible, decentralized creativity. It also produces great wealth for the vast majority of society's members.

Why is this decentralized social order rejected by liberation theologians? Because it rests on a Biblical view of man: "You shall *not* become God." The Bible teaches rather that Christ's perfect humanity, but never His divinity, is imputed to regenerate men by God. No man has a "spark of divinity" in him. Neither man nor his political representative the state is divine. The state cannot become God. A Biblical social order therefore removes most power from the state's bureaucrats. It transfers power to individuals, who are striving to work out their lives on earth in fear and trembling (Philippians 2:12).

Satan's Centralized Hierarchy

In contrast, Satan's social order requires political centralization, so that every detail of each person's life can in principle be monitored by a central elite. This is Satan's substitute for God's omniscience and omnipotence. He cannot see everything, nor can he control everything. He is not God. Satan is a limited creature. He must therefore rely on concentrated political power to achieve his goal to become God. His hierarchy must become total, for he dares not trust men who are self-governing under God. He dares not decentralize. Those who wish to build Satan's kingdom therefore call for compulsory socialistic programs of wealth redistribution as the means for centralizing all other kinds of political control.

This satanic social philosophy is a variant of environmental determinism. Environmental determinism reduces man's personal responsibility before God, which in turn reduces self-government and personal liberty. It offers an excuse to evil people for their continued wrong-doing. The sinner says, in effect: "I'm not depraved; I'm deprived."

Such a view of man transfers authority to elitist scientific planners who supposedly have escaped from the impersonal determining influences of man's environment. They alone are said to be able to reshape social institutions in order to reduce sin by creating a better environment. Understand: to have escaped from the determining environment is to have become trans-human, yet this ability to transcend the environment must be asserted in principle if the central planners are to be freed from the chains of some sort of depersonalized predestinating process. It is the old lure of Satan: "You shall be as God" (Genesis 3:5). It is a system of the divination of the elite. It is a system of bondage from the top down. Yet it is promoted by liberation theology in the name of democracy.

Sovereign God, Responsible People

In contrast, Christianity affirms that it is God who controls all of history, not the impersonal evolutionary forces of nature itself. It is God who regenerates men, not the state. It is not man's impersonal god who holds each person responsible for everything he thinks, says, and does.

Because man's environment is personal and providentially sustained by God, men possess the opportunity to exercise decentralized dominion over nature, since mankind is created in the image of God. Without this image of God in man, mankind could not maintain control over very much of the environment. A person's mind could not be assumed to correspond with his external environment. Humanists who assume that a man's mind does possess this power, especially by means of mathematics and scientific experimentation, cannot explain the origin of this unreasonable connection except by appealing to either miracles or randomness — a Darwinian randomness that somehow has produced cosmic order.[1]

---

1. Gary North, *The Dominion Covenant: Genesis* (Tyler, Texas: Institute for Christian Economics, 1982), Appendix A; "From Cosmic Purposelessness to Humanistic Sovereignty."

A Liberating Gospel

The gospel of Jesus Christ is a gospel of liberation. Liberation in history is therefore just as certain as the triumph of the gospel in history. Liberation is not a side-effect of Christianity; it is an inevitable effect, and a highly desirable one. It will be achieved progressively in time as all rival philosophies of humanism and occultism fall steadily into disrepute. Until then, man's worship of himself, his mind, his institutions, and his ability to plan this world better than God, can and will continue to keep him in moral and institutional bondage.

Those pessimistic Christians who believe that the gospel is historically impotent — that it will not produce saved men and a saved civilization — have no historically relevant answer to the Marxist liberation theologians who preach victory to their followers. The pietists are trying to fight something (a Marxist promise and program for external cultural victory) with nothing (a promise of historical defeat and an antinomian ethical system). *You can't beat something with nothing.*

The Covenant Structure

To covenant with God is to break the chains of Satan's bondage. We must therefore keep God's covenant model in mind. Satan has a rival version of this covenant, and if we are not bound by God's covenant, then we are bound by Satan's. It is never a question of covenant vs. no covenant; it is always a question of *whose* covenant.

First, God is in charge. He created the universe and He sustains it, moment by moment. He is the Sovereign of the universe.

Second, He has established human hierarchies on earth to govern the affairs of men. These are bottom-up appeals courts. Three of them are true covenant institutions: church, family and civil state.

Third, His revealed Word is the source of liberating authority and power. His law is the basis of dominion.

Fourth, there is judgment in history: from God directly and

also from His lawful covenant institutions. These institutions possess lawful authority to execute judgment.

Fifth, those who are faithful to God's covenant, by the grace of God, will inherit the earth. Their victory is assured by God. All other rivals will be disinherited.

This is not mere academic theory. In every institution, and in every area of life, the power of God's covenant is revealed. To give Christians confidence in God and His covenant, I have begun publishing the Biblical Blueprints Series. Christians cannot beat something with nothing; therefore, I am editing books that prove, Bible verse by Bible verse, that the Bible really does have concrete solutions for the major questions of life. We have better answers than all our rivals. Until we believe this, and until we begin taking action in terms of the Biblical requirements, we will remain in bondage.

The road from serfdom begins with repentance: turning around. The road back to Christ's freedom is the road of Christian reconstruction: the rebuilding of every institution and every personal relationship in terms of God's revealed law. Anything less than this is an illusion. Nothing less than this will provide freedom.

Summary

The reasons why it is Christ, and Christ alone, who is the true liberator of the earth are these:

1. All things have been delivered by God into Christ's hands.
2. We are called to take Christ's ethical yoke on ourselves.
3. There is only one way to liberation: subjection to Jesus Christ.
4. We cannot escape hierarchy: either to Christ or to Satan.
5. Civilization is either built in terms of Christianity or is built in terms of Satanism.
6. There is liberty under God's law for individuals.
7. There is also liberty under God's law for societies.
8. Natural law, natural man, and natural freedom are humanist myths.
9. Liberty can only be achieved by obeying God.

10. We must preach the whole counsel of God.

11. Marxist liberation theologians preach revolution, socialism, and bureaucracy.

12. We are to be patient in our present circumstances, yet work faithfully to bring a better world into existence.

13. We are not to choose slavery.

14. Marxism is slavery—the modern world's Egypt.

15. We must not ignore or deny the social evils of our day.

16. We are not to become revolutionaries in an attempt to sweep away social evils.

17. If required, we are to live in the "prison" of social tyranny, but always work to bring Christian civilization into existence.

18. Liberation from sin involves self-government under God's law.

19. The Bible teaches decentralization: a bottom-up hierarchy.

20. Satan imposes a top-down hierarchy.

21. Satan's theology teaches environmental determinism: man is evil because his environment is evil.

22. Such a system relies on elitist planners to perfect the environment, and thereby transform people.

23. Christianity says that individuals are responsible.

24. The process of personal transformation begins in the hearts of men.

25. Liberation is an effect of Christianity.

26. The gospel transforms individuals and institutions.

27. The basis of this transformation is covenantal faithfulness.

28. The covenant has five points.

29. Conformity to the terms of the covenant is the road from serfdom.

BIBLIOGRAPHY

Bahnsen, Greg L. *By This Standard: The Authority of God's Law Today*. Tyler, Texas: Institute for Christian Economics, 1985.

Chilton, David. *The Days of Vengeance: An Exposition of the Book of Revelation*. Ft. Worth, Texas: Dominion Press, 1987.

_____. *Paradise Restored: A Biblical Theology of Dominion*. Ft. Worth, Texas: Dominion Press, 1985.

DeMar, Gary. *Ruler of the Nations: Biblical Blueprints for Government*. Ft. Worth, Texas: Dominion Press, 1987.

Grant, George. *The Changing of the Guard: Biblical Blueprints for Politics*. Ft. Worth, Texas: Dominion Press, 1987.

_____. *In the Shadow of Plenty: Biblical Blueprints for Welfare*. Ft. Worth, Texas: Dominion Press, 1986.

Jordan, James. *Judges: God's War Against Humanism*. Tyler, Texas: Geneva Ministries, 1985.

_____. *The Law of the Covenant: An Exposition of Exodus 21-23*. Tyler, Texas: Institute for Christian Economics, 1984.

North, Gary. *The Dominion Covenant: Genesis*. Tyler, Texas: Institute for Christian Economics, 1982.

_____. *Honest Money: Biblical Blueprints for Money and Banking*. Ft. Worth, Texas: Dominion Press, 1986.

_____. *Inherit the Earth: Biblical Blueprints for Economics*. Ft. Worth, Texas: Dominion Press, 1987.

_____. *Marx's Religion of Revolution: The Doctrine of Creative Destruction*. Nutley, New Jersey: Craig Press, 1968.

161

_____. *Moses and Pharaoh: Dominion Religion vs. Power Religion*. Tyler, Texas: Institute for Christian Economics, 1985.

_____. *Healer of the Nations: Biblical Blueprints for International Relations*. Ft. Worth, Texas: Dominion Press, 1987.

_____. *The Sinai Strategy: Economics and the Ten Commandments*. Tyler, Texas: Institute for Christian Economics, 1987.

_____. *Tools of Dominion: The Case Laws of Exodus*. Tyler, Texas: Institute for Christian Economics, 1987.

_____. *Unconditional Surrender: God's Program for Victory*. Ft. Worth, Texas: Dominion Press, [1981] 1987.

Rushdoony, Rousas J. *The Institutes of Biblical Law*. Nutley, New Jersey: Craig Press, 1973.

Sutton, Ray. *Second Chance: Biblical Blueprints for Divorce and Remarriage*. Ft. Worth, Texas: Dominion Press, 1987.

_____. *That You May Prosper: Dominion by Covenant*. Tyler, Texas: Institute for Christian Economics, 1987.

_____. *Who Owns the Family: God or the State?* Ft. Worth, Texas: Dominion Press, 1986.

Thoburn, Robert L. *The Children Trap: Biblical Blueprints for Education*. Ft. Worth, Texas: Dominion Press, 1986.

SCRIPTURE INDEX

OLD TESTAMENT

NEW TESTAMENT

Matthew

3:14-15	121
3:17	100
4:6	6
5:14	147
5:48	100
6:9-10	24
6:24	19, 39
6:33	40
7:15-20	64
10:27-28	40, 59
11:29-30	17, 19, 149
12:30	21
13:7	96
13:22	95
13:24-43	145
20:15	125, 151
22:37	18
22:38-39	18
25:27	118
28	4
28:18	9
28:18-20	23-24
28:19-20	9

Mark

14:61-64	4

Luke

4	20
4:18-19	14
12:48	118
14:28-30	134
16:19-31	119

John

1:12	56, 62
3:35-36	5
3:36	12

John

8:31-32	1
8:34-36	62
10:30	4
14:6	62
14:15	18, 150
15:13	27
17:15-18	8

Acts

1:9-11	4
7:56	4
17:26-28	62

Romans

1:18	63
2:7	10
3:23	100
5:8-10	18
6:22-23	21
7:23	18, 21
7:25	21
8:18-22	17
8:19-25	11
9:14-23	65
12:2	139
13:10	18

1 Corinthians

1:18	63
2:14-16	63, 150
2:16	140, 141
3	89, 121
3:11-15	10
5	96
6:3	59, 97
7:20-23	48
7:20-24	151-52
7:21-22	110

SUBJECT INDEX

167

WHAT ARE BIBLICAL BLUEPRINTS?

by Gary North

How many times have you heard this one?

"The Bible isn't a textbook of . . ."

You've heard it about as many times as you've heard this one:

"The Bible doesn't provide blueprints for . . ."

The odd fact is that some of the people who assure you of this are Christians. Nevertheless, if you ask them, "Does the Bible have answers for the problems of life?" you'll get an unqualified "yes" for an answer.

Question: If the Bible isn't a textbook, and if it doesn't provide blueprints, then just how, specifically and concretely, does it provide answers for life's problems? Either it answers real-life problems, or it doesn't.

In short: *Does the Bible make a difference?*

Let's put it another way. If a mass revival at last hits this nation, and if millions of people are regenerated by God's grace through faith in the saving work of Jesus Christ at Calvary, will this change be visible in the way the new converts run their lives? Will their politics change, their business dealings change, their families change, their family budgets change, and their church membership change?

In short: Will conversion make a visible difference in our personal lives? If not, why not?

Second, two or three years later, will Congress be voting for a different kind of defense policy, foreign relations policy, environmental policy, immigration policy, monetary policy, and so forth?

177

Will the Federal budget change? If not, why not?

In short: Will conversion to Christ make a visible difference in our civilization? If not, why not?

The Great Commission

What the Biblical Blueprints Series is attempting to do is to outline what some of that visible difference in our culture ought to be. The authors are attempting to set forth, in clear language, *fundamental Biblical principles* in numerous specific areas of life. The authors are not content to speak in vague generalities. These books not only set forth explicit principles that are found in the Bible and derived from the Bible, they also offer specific practical suggestions about what things need to be changed, and how Christians can begin programs that will produce these many changes.

The authors see the task of American Christians just as the Puritans who came to North America in the 1630's saw their task: *to establish a city on a hill* (Matthew 5:14). The authors want to see a Biblical reconstruction of the United States, so that it can serve as an example to be followed all over the world. They believe that God's principles are tools of evangelism, to bring the nations to Christ. The Bible promises us that these principles will produce such good fruit that the whole world will marvel (Deuteronomy 4:5-8). When nations begin to marvel, they will begin to soften to the message of the gospel. What the authors are calling for is *comprehensive revival* — a revival that will transform everything on earth.

In other words, the authors are calling Christians to obey God and take up the Great Commission: to *disciple* (discipline) all the nations of the earth (Matthew 28:19).

What each author argues is that there are God-required principles of thought and practice in areas that some people today believe to be outside the area of "religion." What Christians should know by now is that *nothing* lies outside religion. God is judging all of our thoughts and acts, judging our institutions, and working through human history to bring this world to a final judgment.

We present the case that God offers *comprehensive salvation* — regeneration, healing, restoration, and the obligation of total social reconstruction — because the world is in *comprehensive sin.*

To judge the world it is obvious that God has to have standards. If there were no absolute standards, there could be no earthly judgment, and no final judgment because men could not be held accountable.

(Warning: these next few paragraphs are very important. They are the base of the entire Blueprints series. It is important that you understand my reasoning. I really believe that if you understand it, you will agree with it.)

To argue that God's standards don't apply to everything is to argue that sin hasn't affected and infected everything. To argue that God's Word doesn't give us a revelation of God's requirements for us is to argue that we are flying blind as Christians. It is to argue that there are *zones of moral neutrality* that God will not judge, either today or at the day of judgment, because these zones somehow are *outside His jurisdiction.* In short, "no law-no jurisdiction."

But if God *does* have jurisdiction over the whole universe, which is what every Christian believes, then there must be universal standards by which God executes judgment. The authors of this series argue for God's *comprehensive judgment*, and we declare His *comprehensive salvation.* We therefore are presenting a few of His *comprehensive blueprints.*

The Concept of Blueprints

An architectural blueprint gives us the structural requirements of a building. A blueprint isn't intended to tell the owner where to put the furniture or what color to paint the rooms. A blueprint does place limits on where the furniture and appliances should be put — laundry here, kitchen there, etc. — but it doesn't take away our personal options based on personal taste. A blueprint just specifies what must be done during construction for the building to do its job and to survive the test of time. It gives direction to the contractor. Nobody wants to be on the twelfth floor of a building that collapses.

Today, we are unquestionably on the twelfth floor, and maybe even the fiftieth. Most of today's "buildings" (institutions) were designed by humanists, for use by humanists, but paid for mostly by Christians (investments, donations, and taxes). These "buildings" aren't safe. Christians (and a lot of non-Christians) now are hearing the creaking and groaning of these tottering buildings. Millions of people have now concluded that it's time to: (1) call in a totally new team of foundation and structural specialists to begin a complete renovation, or (2) hire the original contractors to make at least temporary structural modifications until we can all move to safer quarters, or (3) call for an emergency helicopter team because time has just about run out, and the elevators aren't safe either.

The writers of this series believe that the first option is the wise one: Christians need to rebuild the foundations, using the Bible as their guide. This view is ignored by those who still hope and pray for the third approach: God's helicopter escape. Finally, those who have faith in minor structural repairs don't tell us what or where these hoped-for safe quarters are, or how humanist contractors are going to build them any safer next time.

Why is it that some Christians say that God hasn't drawn up any blueprints? If God doesn't give us blueprints, then who does? If God doesn't set the permanent standards, then who does? If God hasn't any standards to judge men by, then who judges man?

The humanists' answer is inescapable: *man* does—autonomous, design-it-yourself, do-it-yourself man. Christians call this man-glorifying religion the religion of humanism. It is amazing how many Christians until quite recently have believed humanism's first doctrinal point, namely, that God has not established permanent blueprints for man and man's institutions. Christians who hold such a view of God's law serve as *humanism's chaplains*.

Men are God's appointed "contractors." We were never supposed to draw up the blueprints, but we *are* supposed to execute them, in history and then after the resurrection. Men have been given dominion on the earth to subdue it for God's glory. "So God created man in His own image; in the image of God He created him; male and female He created them. Then God blessed them, and God said to them, 'Be fruitful and multiply; fill the earth and subdue it; have dominion over the fish of the sea, over the birds of the air, and over every living thing that moves on the earth'" (Genesis 1:27-28).

Christians about a century ago decided that God never gave them the responsibility to do any building (except for churches). That was just what the humanists had been waiting for. They immediately stepped in, took over the job of contractor ("Someone has to do it!"), and then announced that they would also be in charge of drawing up the blueprints. We can see the results of a similar assertion in Genesis, chapter 11: the tower of Babel. Do you remember God's response to that particular humanistic public works project?

Never Be Embarrassed By the Bible

This sounds simple enough. Why should Christians be embarrassed by the Bible? But they *are* embarrassed . . . millions of them. The humanists have probably done more to slow down the spread of the gospel by convincing Christians to be embarrassed by the Bible than by any other strategy they have adopted.

Test your own thinking. Answer this question: "Is God mostly a God of love or mostly a God of wrath?" Think about it before you answer.

It's a trick question. The Biblical answer is: "God is equally a God of love and a God of wrath." But Christians these days will generally answer almost automatically, "God is mostly a God of love, not wrath."

Now in their hearts, they know this answer can't be true. God sent His Son to the cross to die. His own Son! That's how much God hates sin. That's wrath with a capital "W."

But why did He do it? Because He loves His Son, and those who follow His Son. So, you just can't talk about the wrath of God without talking about the love of God, and vice versa. The cross is the best proof we have: God is both wrathful and loving. Without the fires of hell as the reason for the cross, the agony of Jesus Christ on the cross was a mistake, a case of drastic overkill.

What about heaven and hell? We know from John's vision of the day of judgment, "Death and Hades [hell] were cast into the lake of fire. This is the second death. And anyone not found written in the Book of Life was cast into the lake of fire" (Revelation 20:14-15).

Those whose names are in the Book of Life spend eternity with God in their perfect, sin-free, resurrected bodies. The Bible calls this the New Heaven and the New Earth.

Now, which is more eternal, the lake of fire, or the New Heaven and the New Earth? Obviously, they are both eternal. So, God's wrath is equally ultimate with His love throughout eternity. *Christians all admit this,* but sometimes only under extreme pressure. And that is precisely the problem.

For over a hundred years, theological liberals have blathered on and on about the love of God. But when you ask them, "What about hell?" they start dancing verbally. If you press them, they eventually deny the existence of eternal judgment. We *must* understand: they have no doctrine of the total love of God because they have no doctrine of the total wrath of God. They can't really understand what it is that God in His grace offers us in Christ because they refuse to admit what eternal judgment tells us about the character of God.

The doctrine of eternal fiery judgment is by far the most unacceptable doctrine in the Bible, as far as hell-bound humanists are concerned. They can't believe that Christians can believe in such a horror. But we do. We must. This belief is the foundation of Christian evangelism. It is the motivation for Christian foreign missions. We shouldn't be surprised that the God-haters would like us to drop this doctrine. When Christians believe it, they make too much trouble for God's enemies.

So if we believe in this doctrine, the doctrine above all others that ought to embarrass us before humanists, then why do we start to squirm when God-hating people ask us: "Well, what kind of God would require the death penalty? What kind of God would send a plague (or other physical judgment) on people, the way He sent one on the Israelites, killing 70,000 of them, even though they had done nothing wrong, just because David had conducted a military census in peacetime (2 Samuel 24:10-16)? What kind of God sends AIDS?" The proper answer: "The God of the Bible, *my* God."

Compared to the doctrine of eternal punishment, what is some two-bit judgment like a plague? Compared to eternal screaming agony in the lake of fire, without hope of escape, what is the death penalty? The liberals try to embarrass us about these earthly "down payments" on God's final judgment because they want to rid the world of the idea of final judgment. So they insult the character of God, and also the character of Christians, by sneering at the Bible's account of who God is, what He has done in history, and what He requires from men.

Are you tired of their sneering? I know I am.

Nothing in the Bible should be an embarrassment to any Christian. We may not know for certain precisely how some Biblical truth or historic event should be properly applied in our day, but every historic record, law, announcement, prophecy, judgment, and warning in the Bible is the very Word of God, and is not to be flinched at by anyone who calls himself by Christ's name.

We must never doubt that whatever God did in the Old Testament era, the Second Person of the Trinity also did. God's counsel and judgments are not divided. We must be careful not to regard Jesus Christ as a sort of "unindicted co-conspirator" when we read the Old Testament. "For whoever is ashamed of Me and My words in this adulterous and sinful generation, of him the Son of Man also will be ashamed when He comes in the glory of His Father with the holy angels" (Mark 8:38).

My point here is simple. If we as Christians can accept what is a very hard principle of the Bible, that Christ was a blood sacrifice for our individual sins, then we shouldn't flinch at accepting any of the rest of God's principles. As we joyfully accepted His salvation, so we must joyfully embrace all of His principles that affect any and every area of our lives.

The Whole Bible

When, in a court of law, the witness puts his hand on the Bible and swears to tell the truth, the whole truth, and nothing but the truth, so help him God, he thereby swears on the Word of God — the *whole* Word of God, and *nothing but* the Word of God. The Bible is a unit. It's a "package deal." The New Testament doesn't overturn the Old Testament; it's a *commentary* on the Old Testament. It tells us how to use the Old Testament properly in the period after the death and resurrection of Israel's messiah, God's Son.

Jesus said: "Do not think that I came to destroy the Law or the Prophets. I did not come to destroy but to fulfill. For assuredly, I say to you, till heaven and earth pass away, one jot or one tittle will by no means pass from the law till all is fulfilled. Whoever therefore breaks one of the least of these commandments, and teaches men to do so, shall be called least in the kingdom of heaven; but whoever does and teaches them, he shall be called great in the kingdom of heaven" (Matthew 5:17-19). The Old Testament isn't a discarded first draft of God's Word. It isn't "God's Word emeritus."

Dominion Christianity teaches that there are four covenants under God, meaning four kinds of *vows* under God: personal (individual), and the three institutional covenants: ecclesiastical (the church), civil (governments), and family. All other human institutions (business, educational, charitable, etc.) are to one degree or other under the jurisdiction of these four covenants. No single covenant is absolute; therefore, no single institution is all-powerful. Thus, Christian liberty is *liberty under God and God's law.*

Christianity therefore teaches pluralism, but a very special kind of pluralism: plural institutions under God's comprehensive law. It does not teach a pluralism of law structures, or a pluralism of moralities, for as we will see shortly, this sort of ultimate pluralism (as distinguished from *institutional* pluralism) is always either polytheistic or humanistic. Christian people are required to take dominion over the earth by means of all these God-ordained institutions, not just the church, or just the state, or just the family.

The kingdom of God includes every human institution, and every aspect of life, for all of life is under God and is governed by His unchanging principles. All of life is under God and God's principles because God intends to *judge* all of life *in terms of* His principles.

In this structure of *plural governments*, the institutional churches serve as *advisors* to the other institutions (the Levitical function), but the churches can only pressure individual leaders through the threat of excommunication. As a restraining factor on unwarranted church authority, an unlawful excommunication by one local church or denomination is always subject to review by the others if and when the excommunicated person seeks membership elsewhere. Thus, each of the three covenantal institutions is to be run under God, as interpreted by its lawfully elected or ordained leaders, with the advice of the churches, not the compulsion.

Majority Rule

Just for the record, the authors aren't in favor of imposing some sort of top-down bureaucratic tyranny in the name of Christ. The kingdom of God requires a bottom-up society. The bottom-up Christian society rests ultimately on the doctrine of *self*-government under God. It's the humanist view of society that promotes top-down bureaucratic power.

The authors are in favor of evangelism and missions leading to a widespread Christian revival, so that the great mass of earth's inhabitants will place themselves under Christ's protection, and voluntarily use His covenantal principles for self-government. Christian reconstruction begins with personal conversion to Christ and self-government under God's principles, then spreads to others through revival, and only later brings comprehensive changes in civil law, when the vast majority of voters voluntarily agree to live under Biblical blueprints.

Let's get this straight: Christian reconstruction depends on majority rule. Of course, the leaders of the Christian reconstructionist movement expect a majority eventually to accept Christ as savior. If this doesn't happen, then Christians must be content with only partial reconstruction, and only partial blessings from

God. It isn't possible to ramrod God's blessings from the top down, unless you're God. Only humanists think that man is God. All we're trying to do is get the ramrod away from them, and melt it down. The melted ramrod could then be used to make a great grave marker for humanism: "The God That Failed."

The Continuing Heresy of Dualism

Many (of course, not all!) of the objections to the material in this book series will come from people who have a worldview that is very close to an ancient church problem: dualism. A lot of well-meaning Christian people are dualists, although they don't even know what it is.

Dualism teaches that the world is inherently divided: spirit vs. matter, or law vs. mercy, or mind vs. matter, or nature vs. grace. What the Bible teaches is that this world is divided *ethically* and *personally*: Satan vs. God, right vs. wrong. The conflict between God and Satan will end at the final judgment. Whenever Christians substitute some other form of dualism for ethical dualism, they fall into heresy and suffer the consequences. That's what has happened today. We are suffering from revived versions of ancient heresies.

Marcion's Dualism

The Old Testament was written by the same God who wrote the New Testament. There were not two Gods in history, meaning there was no dualism or radical split between the two testamental periods. There is only one God, in time and eternity.

This idea has had opposition throughout church history. An ancient two-Gods heresy was first promoted in the church about a century after Christ's crucifixion, and the church has always regarded it as just that, a heresy. It was proposed by a man named Marcion. Basically, this heresy teaches that there are two completely different law systems in the Bible: Old Testament law and New Testament law (or non-law). But Marcion took the logic of his position all the way. He argued that two law systems means two Gods. The God of wrath wrote the Old Testament, and the God of mercy wrote the New Testament. In short: "two laws-two Gods."

Many Christians still believe something dangerously close to Marcionism: not a two-Gods view, exactly, but a God-who-changed-all-His-rules sort of view. They begin with the accurate teaching that the ceremonial laws of the Old Testament were fulfilled by Christ, and therefore that the *unchanging principles* of Biblical worship are *applied differently* in the New Testament. But then they erroneously conclude that the whole Old Testament system of civil law was dropped by God, and *nothing Biblical was put in its place*. In other words, God created a sort of vacuum for state law.

This idea turns civil law-making over to Satan. In our day, this means that civil law-making is turned over to humanists. *Christians have unwittingly become the philosophical allies of the humanists with respect to civil law.* With respect to their doctrine of the state, therefore, most Christians hold what is in effect a two-Gods view of the Bible.

Gnosticism's Dualism

Another ancient heresy that is still with us is gnosticism. It became a major threat to the early church almost from the beginning. It was also a form of dualism, a theory of a radical split. The gnostics taught that the split is between evil matter and good spirit. Thus, their goal was to escape this material world through other-worldly exercises that punish the body. They believed in *retreat from the world of human conflicts and responsibility.* Some of these ideas got into the church, and people started doing ridiculous things. One "saint" sat on a platform on top of a pole for several decades. This was considered very spiritual. (Who fed him? Who cleaned up after him?)

Thus, many Christians came to view "the world" as something permanently outside the kingdom of God. They believed that this hostile, forever-evil world cannot be redeemed, reformed, and reconstructed. Jesus didn't really die for it, and it can't be healed. At best, it can be subdued by power (maybe). This dualistic view of the world vs. God's kingdom narrowly restricted any earthly manifestation of God's kingdom. Christians who were influenced by gnosticism concluded that God's kingdom refers only to the institutional church. They argued that the institutional church is the *only* manifestation of God's kingdom.

This led to two opposite and equally evil conclusions. *First,* power religionists ("salvation through political power") who accepted this definition of God's kingdom tried to put the institutional church in charge of everything, since it is supposedly "the only manifestation of God's kingdom on earth." To subdue the supposedly unredeemable world, which is forever outside the kingdom, the institutional church has to rule with the sword. A single, monolithic institutional church then gives orders to the state, and the state must without question enforce these orders with the sword. The hierarchy of the institutional church concentrates political and economic power. *What then becomes of liberty?*

Second, escape religionists ("salvation is exclusively internal") who also accepted this narrow definition of the kingdom sought refuge from the evil world of matter and politics by fleeing to hide inside the institutional church, an exclusively "spiritual kingdom," now narrowly defined. They abandoned the world to evil tyrants. *What then becomes of liberty?* What becomes of the idea of God's progressive restoration of all things under Jesus Christ? What, finally, becomes of the idea of Biblical dominion?

When Christians improperly narrow their definition of the kingdom of God, the visible influence of this comprehensive kingdom (both spiritual and institutional at the same time) begins to shrivel up. The first heresy leads to tyranny *by* the church, and the second heresy leads to tyranny *over* the church. Both of these narrow definitions of God's kingdom destroy the liberty of the responsible Christian man, self-governed under God and God's law.

Zoroaster's Dualism

The last ancient pagan idea that still lives on is also a variant of dualism: matter vs. spirit. It teaches that God and Satan, good and evil, are forever locked in combat, and that good never triumphs over evil. The Persian religion of Zoroastrianism has held such a view for over 2,500 years. The incredibly popular "Star Wars" movies were based on this view of the world: the "dark" side of "the force" against its "light" side. In modern versions of this ancient dualism, the "force" is usually seen as itself impersonal: individuals personalize either the dark side or the light side by "plugging into" its power.

There are millions of Christians who have adopted a very pessimistic version of this dualism, though not in an impersonal form. God's kingdom is battling Satan's, and God's is losing. History isn't going to get better. In fact, things are going to get a lot worse externally. Evil will visibly push good into the shadows. The church is like a band of soldiers who are surrounded by a huge army of Indians. "We can't win boys, so hold the fort until Jesus comes to rescue us!"

That doesn't sound like Abraham, Moses, Joshua, Gideon, and David, does it? Christians read to their children one of the children's favorite stories, David and Goliath, yet in their own lives, millions of Christian parents really think that the Goliaths of this world are the unbeatable earthly winners. Christians haven't even picked up a stone.

Until very recently.

An Agenda for Victory

The change has come since 1980. Many Christians' thinking has shifted. Dualism, gnosticism, and "God changed His program midstream" ideas have begun to be challenged. The politicians have already begun to reckon with the consequences. Politicians are the people we pay to raise their wet index fingers in the wind to sense a shift, and they have sensed it. It scares them, too. It should.

A new vision has captured the imaginations of a growing army of registered voters. This new vision is simple: it's the old vision of Genesis 1:27-28 and Matthew 28:19-20. It's called *dominion*.

Four distinct ideas must be present in any ideology that expects to overturn the existing view of the world and the existing social order:

A doctrine of ultimate truth (permanence)
A doctrine of providence (confidence)
Optimism toward the future (motivation)
Binding comprehensive law (reconstruction)

The Marxists have had such a vision, or at least those Marxists who don't live inside the bureaucratic giants called the Soviet Union and Red China. The radical (please, not "fundamentalist") Muslims of Iran also have such a view.

Now, for the first time in over 300 years, Bible-believing Christians have rediscovered these four points in the theology of Christianity. For the first time in over 300 years, a growing number of Christians are starting to view themselves as an army on the move. This army will grow. This series is designed to help it grow. And grow tougher.

The authors of this series are determined to set the agenda in world affairs for the next few centuries. We know where the permanent answers are found: in the Bible, and *only* in the Bible. We believe that we have begun to discover at least preliminary answers to the key questions. There may be better answers, clearer answers, and more orthodox answers, but they must be found in the Bible, not at Harvard University or on the CBS Evening News.

We are self-consciously firing the opening shot. We are calling the whole Christian community to join with us in a very serious debate, just as Luther called them to debate him when he nailed the 95 theses to the church door, over four and a half centuries ago.

It is through such an exchange of ideas by those who take the Bible seriously that a nation and a civilization can be saved. There are now 5 billion people in the world. If we are to win our world (and these billions of souls) for Christ we must lift up the message of Christ by becoming the city on the hill. When the world sees the blessings by God upon a nation run by His principles, the mass conversion of whole nations to the Kingdom of our Lord will be the most incredible in of all history.

If we're correct about the God-required nature of our agenda, it will attract a dedicated following. It will produce a social transformation that could dwarf the Reformation. This time, we're not limiting our call for reformation to the institutional church.

This time, we mean business.

Dr. Gary North
Institute for Christian Economics
P.O. Box 8000
Tyler, TX 75711

Dear Dr. North:

I read about your organization in your book, *Liberating Planet Earth*. I understand that you publish several newsletters that are sent out for six months free of charge. I would be interested in receiving them:

    ☐ *Biblical Economics Today*
       Christian Reconstruction
       and *Covenant Renewal*

Please send any other information you have concerning your program.

_____
name

_____
address

_____
city, state, zip

_____
area code and phone number

☐ Enclosed is a tax-deductible donation to help meet expenses.

Jesus said to "Occupy till I come." But if Christians don't control the territory, they can't occupy it. They get tossed out into cultural "outer darkness," which is just exactly what the secular humanists have done to Christians in the 20th century: in education, in the arts, in entertainment, in politics, and certainly in the mainline churches and seminaries. Today, the humanists are "occupying." But they won't be for long. *Backward, Christian Soldiers?* shows you why. This is must reading for all Christians as a supplement to the *Biblical Blueprints Series*. You can obtain a copy by sending $1.00 (a $5.95 value) to:

> Institute for Christian Economics
> P.O. Box 8000
> Tyler, TX 75711

---

name

---

address

---

city, state, zip

---

area code and phone number

The *Biblical Blueprints Series* is a multi-volume book series that gives Biblical solutions for the problems facing our culture today. Each book deals with a specific topic in a simple, easy to read style such as economics, government, law, crime and punishment, welfare and poverty, taxes, money and banking, politics, the environment, retirement, and much more.

Each book can be read in one evening and will give you the basic Biblical principles on each topic. Each book concludes with three chapters on how to apply the principles in your life, the church and the nation. Every chapter is summarized so that the entire book can be absorbed in just a few minutes.

As you read these books, you will discover hundreds of new ways to serve God. Each book will show you ways that you can start to implement God's plan in your own life. As hundreds of thousands join you, and millions more begin to follow the example set, a civilization can be changed.

Why will people change their lives? Because they will see God's blessings on those who live by His Word (Deuteronomy 4:6-8).

Each title in the *Biblical Blueprints Series* is available in a deluxe paperback edition for $7.95, or a classic leatherbound edition for $15.95.

The following titles are scheduled for publication:

- Liberating Planet Earth: An Introduction to Biblical Blueprints
- Ruler of the Nations: Biblical Blueprints for Governments
- Who Owns the Family?: Biblical Blueprints for Family/State Relations
- In the Shadow of Plenty: Biblical Blueprints for Welfare and Poverty
- Honest Money: Biblical Blueprints for Money and Banking
- The Children Trap: Biblical Blueprints for Education
- Inherit the Earth: Biblical Blueprints for Economics
- The Changing of the Guard: Biblical Blueprints for Political Action
- Healer of the Nations: Biblical Blueprints for International Relations
- Second Chance: Biblical Blueprints for Divorce and Remarriage

Please send more information concerning this program.

---

name

---

address

---

city, state, zip

Dominion Press • P.O. Box 8204 • Ft. Worth, TX 76124